PLANTS THAT SPAN THE SEASONS

PLANTS THAT SPAN THE SEASONS

Roger Wilson

GUILD OF MASTER CRAFTSMAN PUBLICATIONS LTD

Dedication

Jan, for twelve years, thank you.

First published 2000 by
Guild of Master Craftsman Publications Ltd,
166 High Street, Lewes,
East Sussex BN7 1XU

ISBN 1 86108 167 7

A catalogue record of this book is available from the British Library.

Editors: Andy Charman and Nicola Wright
Designer: Philip Jones at limegreenhorse.com
Line illustrations: Richard Nash
Typeface: Times
Colour separation: Viscan Graphics P.L. (Singapore)
Printed and bound by Kyodo Printing (Singapore)
under the supervision of MRM Graphics, Winslow, Buckinghamshire, UK

10 9 8 7 6 5 4 3 2 1

Picture acknowledgements:
Pages vi, 2, 4, 6, 7 (bottom right), 11 (top left & bottom left), 12 (top right), 16, 17, 18 (right), 22, 25, 26, 2728, 29, 30, 31, 32, 33, 34, 35, 36, 37 (left), 38, 39, 41, 42, 44, 45, 47, 49, 50, 51, 52, 53, 55, 56, 57, 58, 59, 61, 62, 63, 64 (left), 65 (right), 67, 68, 69, 70, 72, 76, 77, 88 (left), 92, 97, 98, 99, 108, 111, 112 (right), 113, 116 (bottom left), 117, 124 A-Z Botanical Photographic Library; pages 7 (left & top right), 8 (right), 10, 11 (right), 15, 20, 21, 37 (right), 43, 46, 64 (right), 65 (left), 71, 73, 75, 79, 80, 81, 82, 84, 85, 88 (right), 90 (bottom), 91 (left), 94 (left), 95, 96, 98, 100, 105 (right), 107, 109, 112 (left), 114, 115, 120, 121, 123 Harry Smith Horticultural Picture Library; pages 14 (right), 18 (left), 54, 60, 78, 87 (bottom left), 93 (left), 94 (right), 103, 106, 118, 122 (right), 131 Roger Wilson; pages 91 (right), 92 (bottom), 102, 104, 116 (top left) Hamdene Photographics; pages iv & v, 8 (left), 9 (left), 14 (left), 24, 87 (top left), 89, 90 (top right), 93 (right), 101, 105 (top left), 110, 119, 122 (left), 138 GMC Publications.

CONTENTS

INTRODUCTION

One thing that always intrigues me when I am giving gardening advice is that people expect plants to grow precisely as the books etc. describe. Whenever someone complains at my garden centre about their clematis not flowering in June, for instance, I point out that plants cannot read. This almost flippant answer hides an important point. This is that books etc. can only advise; you are the only person that will really get to know your garden, and, as we all know, things don't always 'go by the book'.

Once, during a garden club talk in Birmingham, I made the normal cultural comment on hyacinths: they are not hardy and need lifting for winter storage. A few members of the audience piped up with the fact that hyacinths were not only growing outdoors all year round in their gardens, but were also propagating themselves. We discussed the matter, and there were good horticultural reasons why the plants were so happy. I hope this book will not only give you some instant pleasure, but some good advice and some ideas too, to help your garden be more of what you want.

Most gardeners want to maximize the use of their garden, whether that be their vegetable production, outdoor living space or creating the garden of their dreams. This book is about making the most of your garden by the judicious use of plants which will give more than one period of interest a year. Sometimes a plant with a long flowering period will be included (e.g. *Potentilla fruticosa* 'Elizabeth'), but this book focuses on plants that provide different features at different times of the year. This often means a spring, or summer, flowering plant, which then follows with berries or autumn colour. Some plants which provide all-year-round interest are also discussed. All plants mentioned will survive most winters outside.

The idea of using these plants is to create the maximum effect in your garden for the minimum effort. Much as gardening is a great pleasure, you need to have time to enjoy the fruits of your labours. Also, many people do not have time to garden in the traditional manner. Thus, the majority of plants mentioned in this book require minimal attention after the first year of planting.

The plants listed generally allow for modern housing trends, with gardens getting smaller, as you may not have enough room to grow plants for features at all times of the year. It may take a little more effort to choose the right plants but, with the help of this book, you can create a garden which is easy to tend that will spectacularly span the seasons. Enjoy.

Making the Most of Your Plants

MAKING THE MOST OF YOUR PLANTS

This section of the book will give you some general guidance on preparing an area for planting, about plants and their selection for your garden. For more experienced gardeners, I hope you pick up a few useful hints and tips, possibly seeing why certain plants haven't done as expected, nor stayed as healthy as when they came from the garden centre!

Your Soil

The type of soil your garden has is crucial to what sort of plants you can grow. This is because plants have adapted themselves to certain soil conditions: the pH (acidity), the level of nutrients and moisture content, for example. There are lots of factors involved, and many interlink; indeed this area is still a matter for a great deal of research. For instance, we do not really understand how plants extract nutrients from the soil. However, we gardeners can approach the subject in a more pragmatic way and simply follow the requirements of a particular plant.

One key factor that gardeners *can* alter is the level of organic matter. The next time you visit an established woodland, try digging into the soil a little. It will be black and 'rich'. This is because over the years the leaves have rotted back into the soil, improving its structure. Organic matter not only helps the soil structure (and so the oxygen level, or aeration), but also increases the soil's ability to hold water and nutrients. A soil rich in organic matter will support a much wider range of plants more easily than a similar soil to which no organic matter has been added.

Many gardeners use fertilizers, such as Growmore, to increase nutrients, but do not add organic matter. I always recommend, when planting 'permanent' plants (as opposed to bedding plants or annuals), that you add copious amounts of organic matter as a matter of course, whether it is garden compost, rotted manure, or stuff bought from a garden centre. Other than mulching (see Planting and Aftercare, page 19), it is the only opportunity you have to change the nature of the soil in any major way.

Preparation

Another item to consider when you are preparing your soil for planting is drainage. As with the organic matter, if your planting is to be permanent, this is the only chance you will have to improve the soil effectively. If the soil is heavy and/or clay-like in texture, adding coarse grit as well as organic matter will improve things no end. A lot of people make the mistake of not being enthusiastic enough. To make a real, permanent difference, I highly recommend a form of double digging (see illustration overleaf). Starting at one end of the area you are wanting to improve, dig a trench one and a half to two spade widths' wide, and a spade depth (or spit) deep, transferring the soil to a wheelbarrow. Then liberally cover the bottom of the trench with organic matter and a thin layer of grit. Fork this into the bottom of the trench. Then dig the adjacent soil on top of the mixture you have just forked in, thus creating a new trench beside the original one.

You may well have to add items to the soil as you move it. Unless you have a light soil, you will have a lot of lumps; pour more organic matter and grit on and around them and break them down with a garden fork, mixing the added materials at the same time. On light soils, fork a thin layer of organic matter into the soil. Repeat this procedure until you have dug your patch, then empty the wheelbarrow into the trench at the other end, adding organic matter (and grit) as necesary. This all adds up to a lot of hard work, but it will make gardening this patch a lot easier in the future.

This method can also be applied on a small scale in established beds. If you are digging between plants or replacing one of them with a trowel, add organic matter when possible. On large areas, you may consider hiring a Rotavator, or even paying a landscape contractor to rotavate for you. I am not a great fan of Rotavators. They are dangerous, noisy things, but if you do choose this method, cover the ground to a minimum of 7cm (3in) with the organic matter (and grit where appropriate) and rotavate it in. Then apply another layer and rotavate this in as well. The double application will result in a good spread through the soil. With both soil improvement methods, the height of the soil will increase because of the increase in air spaces and the materials you have added. This is beneficial when you are trying to

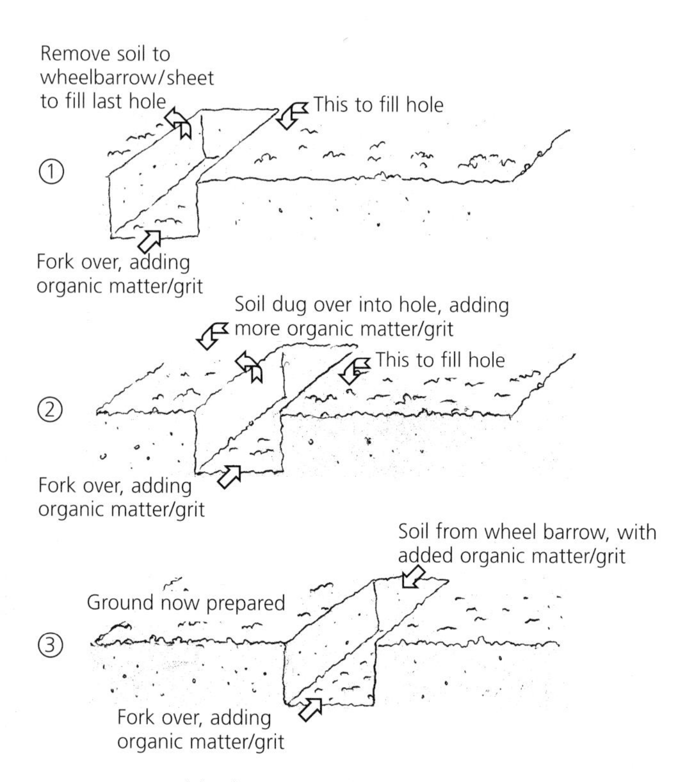

Double digging method

improve drainage. One of the beds in my garden prepared in this way was 30cm (12in) higher than the lawn beside it. The bed was dug as described for two consecutive winters. A lot of organic matter was added and, because it was a heavy, clay soil, copious amounts of coarse grit. Now, nearly six years later, it is still about 20cm (8in) higher than the lawn, which was not improved. The various shrubs, apple trees and vegetables have all thrived.

What can you grow?

One area over which you have little control is your soil's pH (acidity/alkalinity). It is possible to alter pH on a temporary basis, but for easy gardening it is better to select plants which like your soil's pH in the first place. It is a quick matter to find out what pH your soil is. You can buy single tests very cheaply. For larger gardens I would recommend multiple tests from different areas. All garden centres, and some high-street shops, will stock these pH tests. There are also pH meters available. Some garden centres will test your soil for you, if you leave them a sample. A pH of between 6.5 and 8 will mean that you can grow the vast majority of garden plants, particularly if you are willing to carry out some aftercare. A good example of this is hydrangea. Most hydrangeas will produce pink flowers in an alkaline soil (i.e. pH higher than 7). You can make them blue by using hydrangea colourant, or sulphate of aluminium (both are available at gardening shops). These fertilizers add a lot of aluminium to the soil, which hydrangeas have difficulty extracting from alkaline soils. It is the aluminium which makes the flowers blue. A lot of white-flowering plants will get a pinkish tinge to the flowers in alkaline soils for a similar reason.

A pH of less than 6.5 means you will be looking at plants like rhododendrons, heathers, azaleas, etc. These are ericaceous plants. A pH of more than 8 means plants like lilacs, laburnum and daphnes. It is a good idea is to look at other gardens in your area; this will give you an idea of what you are likely to be able to grow. If you don't know what a particular plant is, you can always ask! If you are able to obtain a piece of the plant, the RHS and most garden centres will assist with its identification. Try to get as many different parts of the plant as possible: leaf,

Pink hydrangea

flower, stem and so on. If your soil is only just below pH 7, and you wish to grow ericaceous plants, then I would recommend either sulphate of iron, Miracid or Sequestrene as fertilizers to help you. I particularly like Miracid, because it

Blue hydrangea

contains a soil acidifier, as well as the extra iron that these plants find difficult to absorb from the soil. All of them should be readily available from good gardening shops. There are more comprehensive lists of plants for low and high pH soils later in this book.

If your soil has a fairly extreme pH (i.e. lower than 5.5 or higher than 8.5), then your plants, and thus the flowering/interest period could be quite limited. For instance, the vast majority of ericaceous plants flower in the spring, but with careful selection you can increase the number of colourful months. You can also seek out some of the more unusual plants if your garden provides the right conditions for them to grow. You may also have to focus more on structure, with contrasting foliage, for example, rather than just flowers. I have seen a garden that was just ferns and some bulbs, hardly any 'colour' except green, and it was delightful. It also provided interest most of the year, because some of the ferns were evergreen and the bulbs well chosen.

A mixed border of rhododendrons and azaleas

Laburnum in full flower provides a spectacular display

Container gardening

One way around the problem of your soil being the wrong pH for the plant you want to grow is to use containers with a proprietary compost. Garden soil is not suitable for pots because it does not drain freely or hold nutrients well

enough. It can be made suitable with sand, organic matter, and so on, but this is likely to work out more expensive than buying the compost ready made. It is certainly more work – no doubt about that! If you can grow houseplants, there is no reason why you should not make a success of container gardening.

Contrasting foliage adds form and interest

For acid-loving plants, you can buy ericaceous compost; for virtually all other plants a potting or container compost is what you need. A multi-purpose compost will do the job, but the reason they are cheaper is that they contain less food than the specialist composts and are not so well designed. You will get much better results more easily with the correct compost.

For certain plants, such as roses, lilies and conifers I prefer a John Innes compost, which is **loam**-based (loam is an important constituent of soil), but the peat-based composts mentioned above will be fine. John Innes compost is available in various forms. The specialist ones are the ericaceous and seed composts. The others are numbered 1, 2 and 3. The numbers refer to the amount of fertilizer or nutrients in them. For autumn and winter, numbers 1 and 2 are best; for spring use number 3. Number 1 is also used for potting up seedlings. If you have trouble with containers drying out, it would be worth trying a John Innes compost.

Containers allow you to choose your soil type

When planting a patio or garden pot, always leave the compost level about 2.5cm (1in) below the rim. This allows you to flood the top of the pot when watering. You should always water pots until the water runs freely from the bottom drainage hole or holes. Any pot kept outside must have drainage holes, unless you are growing pond plants! You should also put a layer of gravel, stone or other coarse material in the bottom of the pot before you add the compost; this is also for drainage. Some plants that are good in containers like to be moist – hostas, for example – so it may be a good idea to leave out the gravel layer if you find they are drying out too easily.

Another suggestion for any size of garden is a watering system, such as micro-drip. These are excellent for pots and greenhouses. As with soil preparation, installing one creates a bit of work initially, but the result is more deckchair time later. Garden centres should stock such products and be able to offer advice. A watering system in conjunction with a timer can make gardening very easy and save worry when it comes to being away from home for a while.

If you have the room, container gardening is a good way to create bursts of colour, and when one plant has finished its display, you swap that pot for another and put the finished one in a less conspicuous part of the garden. National Trust properties, parks and gardens do this all the time, which is why you rarely see a poor container display in these places. One of my favourite bursts of colour which lasts all spring is a container planted with snowdrops, daffodils and tulips.

Hosta fortunei 'Aureo-Marginata' growing in a pot

By careful selection of the varieties – the main area to watch is the daffodil to tulip flowering time – you can achieve four to five months of colour. One reason this selection works so well is that the different bulbs like different planting depths: they are planted – in the autumn – in layers. You should arrange the bulbs quite densely, almost touching, and try to avoid putting a bulb directly above another, although even that doesn't really matter. As a general guide, the tulips should be planted deepest (i.e. first in the pot as you fill it), then the daffodils above, and finally the snowdrops on top. Virtually all bulbs are sold in packets these days which will tell you how deep the bulbs need to be planted. If the tulips and daffodils need a similar depth, put the tulips deepest.

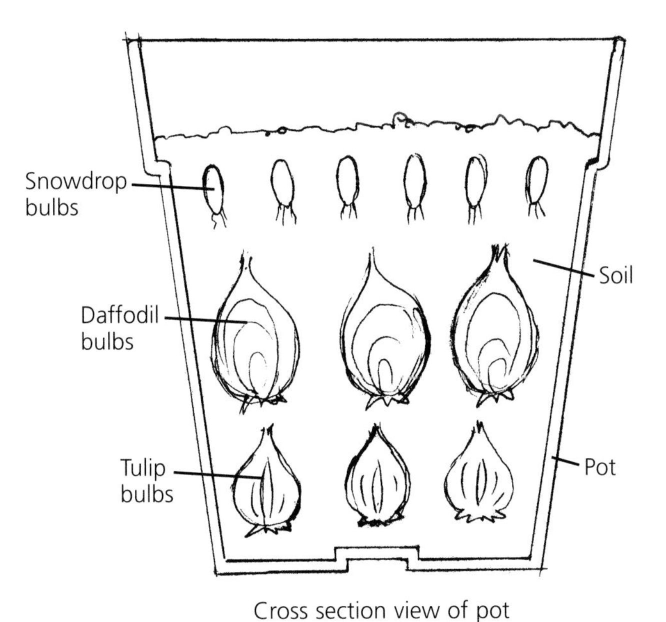

Cross section view of pot

Container planted with snowdrops, daffodils and tulips

A Background to Plants

Plant properties

Anyone can recognize a tree, but how would you define what one is? The differences between different sorts of plants can be very important horticulturally. This section offers an introduction to what the differences are and what that means to the gardener. More definitions can be found in the Glossary.

Hardy cotoneasters covered with snow

The most important term to remember is **hardiness**. If a plant is hardy, it will generally survive the winter outdoors. You should pay close attention when purchasing heathers and perennials because these groups of plants can vary quite widely in their ability to live through British winters. If a plant is not hardy, it should have a label which clearly states this. An important point to note, however, is that you might have a more sheltered area (a south-facing wall, for instance) that would allow a more tender plant to be grown successfully. Also, that giving a plant it's ideal conditions will increase its likelihood of survival. A good example of this is *Actinidia kolomikta,* a climbing plant. *Actinidia kolomikta* is certainly not hardy in the north of the UK, but if it is grown on a south-facing wall, it will withstand all but the severest winters. *Actinidia kolomikta* will die readily, even in the south of the country, if it is not given a good, well-draining soil.

Actinidia growing on a south-facing wall

If the forecast is for an extreme cold snap, you can wrap tender plants in protection fleece, which is available from garden centres, or even in old newspapers or sheets as a temporary measure. The fleece can be left on a plant for extended periods, but the substitutes must be removed at least every other day or the plant is likely to go mouldy. These barriers will protect the plant from a few extra degrees of frost, more if you devise a method of holding the material away from the actual plant to create an air gap of at least 3–4cm (1–1½in). A wooden frame is most suitable, even one made from bamboo canes. Again, you could look at other gardens in your area or ask advice at your garden centre.

One of the most important decisions to make when selecting a plant is whether it should be **deciduous** or **evergreen**. The latter, as you'd expect, is always 'green' or a shade thereof; deciduous is the technical term for a plant that drops its leaves for the winter. The colour of autumn leaves before they drop is one of my favourite sights and it is easy to introduce into

Plant wrapped in a fleece to protect it from the cold

your garden. Small trees are probably best for this, but many shrubs are suitable, and some perennials also give good autumn colour.

Acer palmatum provides stunning autumn colour

Types of plants

There are many different kinds of plants, including bulbs, cacti, epiphytes, perennials, succulents, shrubs, trees, alpines and conifers. Some of these terms come from their scientific description, some are horticultural and others colloquial; there is not always agreement even among the 'experts', so there are grey areas. This explains why, at the garden centre, you may find a certain plant among the shrubs, being sold as an alpine, and in the herb section as well – rosemary (*Rosmarinus officinalis* 'Miss Jessopp's Upright' variety), for example. A local garden centre stocks it as a shrub in a 3 litre (9in diameter) pot and as a herb in a 0.25 litre (3½in diameter) pot. It is also sold, at garden shows particularly, as an alpine because it will thrive in the conditions that alpines enjoy. (For a definition of the different kinds of plants, see the Glossary on page 126. Any word in bold will be listed.)

Rosmarinus officinalis 'Miss Jessopp's Upright'

Many of the words that are regularly used in horticultural circles to describe plants have specific meanings. **Prostrate** means a plant which grows close to the ground; *Cotoneaster humifusus,* for example. **Fastigiate** means a narrow, pointed, upright plant such as *Juniperus scopulorum* 'Skyrocket' and *Prunus* 'Amanogawa'. You may find that you like a particular style of plant, and wish to grow more of them, but you should bear in mind that you need other shapes and sizes to create contrast, or your garden will become too uniform and boring. Again, look at other people's gardens, National Trust properties, and so on, for inspiration. Also, do not be afraid to experiment; if you get it wrong, the worst thing that can happen is that you will lose a plant or two. Usually you can rescue a plant by moving it elsewhere, or just feed or prune it more often than is ideal. If you like thinking about style and structure, you may wish to become more involved with the overall design of your garden. There is more about this later in the section on selecting plants, which begins on page 13.

Cotoneaster humifusus covering the ground

One term that a gardener should be aware of is **ground cover**. A plant that gives good ground cover has two main attributes: it is easy to look after and has dense foliage to minimize weeds. Plants that fit this description are often used on landscaping projects, on roadsides, roundabouts and airports, for example, and so are relatively cheap and freely available. It is common for ground-cover plants to be evergreen, but not exclusively. One of my favourite plants, *Viburnum opulus* 'Compactum', is deciduous and gives excellent ground cover. If you underplant it with crocus and dwarf narcissii (daffodils), you will have 'show' all year round; the viburnum flowers in late spring, and gives a lovely display of autumn colour . See page 80 for further information on this plant.

Juniperus scopulorum 'Skyrocket' reaching for the sky

Viburnum opulus 'Compactum' is deciduous

A lot of horticulturists include within the definition of ground cover that the plant is low growing, even prostrate, but this height restriction is unnecessary. Rhododendrons can be enormous but, because they fulfil the above criteria, they are generally good ground-cover plants. Most lists of ground-cover plants do not include taller ones, so it is worth remembering them when you are at the garden centre.

Plant names

The last point to cover in this section is the naming of plants. Many plants have a common name, but the horticulture industry uses Latin names to ensure that everyone is discussing the same plant. Common names vary dramatically even in different parts of the country, let alone globally. Any system that tried to control common names would create as many problems as currently exist with Latin nomenclature. Using Latin also means that the native language of the gardener does not interfere with effective communication.

There are two main parts to a plant's Latin name: the first part refers to the **genus** to which it belongs and the second refers to the particular **species**. We often use the genus name in common speech: rhododendron or potentilla, for example, but this is only useful when the genus describes a range of broadly similar plants. The various species within a genus may look completely different. As the science of genetics develops, plants are being grouped by their genetic similarity. This causes problems when unexpected links are found and plants have to be re-named, making books out of date. Plants are re-named for other reasons also, but people tend to remember the names that have been in use for a long time. This explains why you sometimes find a plant with another Latin name – the older name – in brackets after its current one. Some books also give you a plant's Latin family name. Roses belong to the *Rosa* genus in the *Rosaceae* family. The family name is not generally very useful to the gardener, but it becomes of interest in the actual study of plants.

Selecting Plants

Garden design

Before discussing the selection of plants in more detail, I would like to raise the topic of garden design. If you wish, you can choose to employ a professional landscape designer. Unfortunately, it is hard to be sure of the advice you are given because there is no trade association guaranteeing quality, and there are a lot of 'cowboys' out there. In Britain, the Yellow Pages is a good place to start. If you want construction work as well, look for the letters BALI which stand for the British Association of Landscape Industries. You may pay a little more, but it is unlikely that remedial work will be required later. A recommendation from a friend or colleague can be helpful, particularly if they are knowledgeable, or you could ask your local garden centre if they can recommend anyone. With a reputable designer or contractor, you should not have to pay any money 'up-front', though interim payments may be required, particularly for larger projects.

Whether using a designer or doing it yourself, it pays to know what you want from your garden. Do you need an area for children to play in? Do you want a vegetable plot and compost heap and if so, do you want to hide them from the house? Is a patio on your list of requirements, and what size should it be? If you enjoy large, family barbecues, how much and what sort of furniture do you need to allow for? It may be helpful, particularly if you are discussing it with a designer or partner, to draw a plan, even if it is only a rough one. The old saying 'a picture is worth a thousand words' is certainly relevant here and in this way you can be sure that you are visualizing the same thing. If you can, you may even do three-dimensional sketches to get an idea of what it will look like in 'real life'.

There are two main aspects to garden design: hard and soft landscaping, and they should complement each other. Hard landscaping consists of the paving, fencing, walls and so on. Soft landscaping includes the plants, lawn and

A well-designed garden

Gravel used as mulch on flower beds

soil. Ideally, the proportion of hard to soft landscape should be 2:1 (or 1:2) in any given area, but do not get too concerned with this if you like the way your garden looks. The boundary between the two can become blurred by growing plants on walls, using gravel as a mulch on flowerbeds, and so on. There are many books which concentrate on garden design alone, but make sure you study them before you buy, because they are not always useful for general gardening.

Overall planting scheme

If you are planning a whole bed, or even the entire garden, you should 'mix and match' plant types to get seasonal variation (autumn leaf colour, winter bark, etc), some structure (i.e. evergreen plants) and colour in the winter, and get as wide a flowering period as possible across the display. You may bias the display towards the summer because that is when you are likely to spend most time in the garden, but if you have nothing at all for the winter, there will be little to tempt you outside when the weather *is* pleasant. One garden I designed is approximately 8 x 8m (26 x 26ft). Half of this is lawn (for the clothes line!); in the rest of the space there are flowers, catkins or other features, such as foliage, bark, autumn colour, creating interest all year round. This was achieved by careful selection of plants according to when they provided their interest (approximately), their size (to some degree) and whether they were suitable for the particular spot in the garden. The heavy clay soil encouraged me to use plants that like moist ground, such as primulas, even though lots of organic matter and grit had been dug in over the years. Because of that improvement, I was able to use some plants that liked free-draining soil, such as *Genista lydia*. On one small bed by the patio, I removed the soil completely and added grit and organic matter to the bottom of the hole and then filled it with potting compost. This enabled some much-desired alpines to spread out over the edge of the paving and into the gaps left between the slabs. More are in pots on the patio, along with a couple of ericaceous plants that the garden is totally unsuitable for.

A plant's size is only an influence to some degree. This is because the sizes given in plant books (including this one) are for the mature plant. It can take them many years, decades, or even centuries to achieve this ultimate size, so growth rate is an important factor in any decision. 'Fast-growing' usually means big! A

Raised alpine bed

× *Cupressocyparis leylandii* makes a good screen

good example of this is the much-maligned × *Cupressocyparis leylandii*. This tree is often used for hedging or screening because it is one of the fastest growing plants. However, if it is not trimmed, it will grow into a large, evergreen tree. There are some excellent specimens at Bedgebury Pinetum in Kent, which are about 30m (100ft) high. As can be seen in the picture above, size can be controlled by pruning, or trimming if it is a hedge. Using a plant that will be too big for what you want it to do in your garden will create work, but this is never too onerous; at worst it need only be an annual task.

To minimize the workload, you should aim to avoid a plant that will be significantly larger than the space you have, or a plant with a very high growth rate. I control a *Fuchsia magellanica* with a brutal prune each autumn/winter. Instead of having a height and spread of 3m (10ft), I keep it to 1.8m (6ft) high and 1m (3ft) wide, trained around my water butt. There are also two plants that I plan to remove in about another five to ten years, because they will get too big, but they will be fine until then. At the price I paid for them, if they live another five years they will have cost me less than 50 pence a year – well worth it for the pleasure they have given me.

Choosing specific plants

The key requirement for easy gardening is to use a plant that will grow in the conditions provided by your garden. The two factors to consider are light level and soil. Soil has been discussed in the previous section; if you know what your soil is like, then you are in a good position to select plants with confidence.

The reason why light level is so important is that plants have evolved their ability to photosynthesize to this factor. Plants are green because the substance in their cells which turns light into food, chorophyll, is that colour. From this it follows that plants that can tolerate lower light levels are a darker green (and usually 'glossy') and plants that are not so green (bluish, for example) require more light. This is a useful general guideline, but Mother Nature being what she is, it is only a guide! Any good description of a plant will tell you what level of light it prefers.

The best way of assessing the light level in a particular part of your garden is to see how much direct sun it gets during the course of a day. 'Full sun' defines an area that is exposed all day; 'partial shade' refers to one that only gets the sun for part of the day (usually morning or evening – partial-shade plants generally do not like midday sun). It could also be an area where the level of shading is quite low, beneath the canopy of a birch tree, for example. 'Full shade' means no direct sun at all. Our understanding of shade is very subjective, because the human eye only works in contrasts, not absolute light levels. That is why I recommend to gardening beginners that they work mostly on the amount of direct sun during the course of a day. As always, if you are unsure, your local garden centre will help, but be prepared to answer questions yourself.

Ceanothus 'Cascade' likes full sun

One of the best ways of selecting plants is to visit garden centres, National Trust properties and other gardens open to the public at the time of year that you are wanting a feature or colour. Some gardens are particularly useful because they label their plants.

If you do have a particular sort of plant in mind for your garden, it could well be worth visiting a specialist nursery, many of which operate a mail-order service. Plants are usually despatched in the autumn or winter because this is the best time to lift and transplant 'field-grown' plants. You should order your plants as soon as you can, because most specialist nurseries are small businesses and only grow small quantities of any one plant to minimize their risks; if you wait until the autumn or winter, they are likely to have sold out of their popular lines. If you are lucky, you may well find a specialist grower who does some container-grown stock for their visitors and local garden centres. However, do not assume that because you are buying direct from the grower that the plants will be cheaper; they can be, but specialists tend to grow the more unusual varieties of plants and they cost more. This is fine if you are getting a noticeably different plant, but many varieties can look quite similar to each other. This is particularly true of roses, fuchsias and geraniums.

I enjoy the process of seeking out and selecting plants, perusing the books, making notes and lists, and visiting homes and gardens. I often take photographs of ideas, borders or plants I like to give me inspiration when I am back home. Of course, new ideas can be incorporated into an existing layout. One of the joys of gardening is the continual progress of growth, learning and change, even if only to make space for the latest plant to take your fancy at the garden centre.

Buying plants

Before you visit a garden centre or nursery to buy plants, it is helpful to have some idea of what you need. The whole garden retailing industry started in the early 1960s with the development of economical plant-production methods using plastic pots. Before this, mail-order nurseries, and small, local nurseries that dug your selected plant out of the field were the norm. Most garden centres will have a range of plants displayed in their grounds; they may even have display gardens. For new gardeners, seeing plants in flower, and being able to plant them in flower is one of the great benefits of modern horticulture. A container-grown plant can be planted at any time of the year, as long as the ground is not frozen. For easiest aftercare, autumn planting is best, followed by spring.

A rose nursery

The three main factors affecting the price of a plant are how exclusive it is (to the retailer or grower), how easy it is to grow to a saleable size, and the size of the plant when you purchase it. The reason that ease of growing is important is twofold: fussy plants require a more precise set of conditions and fewer are likely to reach saleable quality. The size of the plant you purchase is again a twofold point: a slow-growing plant may take anything up to five years to become a saleable plant, whereas a fast-growing plant could well be sold within a year of being propagated. Secondly, the longer a crop stays with a grower, the more risks, and costs, are invested in the plants.

You may wish to purchase a large (specimen) plant, for the instant effect it will create. A good example of this is *Ajuga reptans*, a spreading, ground-cover perennial. You could buy this plant in a 9cm (3½in) pot for £1.79 in 1998, or in a 2 litre (3½ pt) pot for £4.95. The former is about six months old, the latter about two years. However, in the long run, a smaller plant will often out-grow a larger one of the same variety planted at the same time. How soon obviously depends on the difference in size, the aftercare and the type of plant. Smaller plants tend to need less aftercare. These reasons, together with the cost, are why smaller plants are usually used on landscaping projects, though larger plants may be incorporated for 'prestige' locations to give some maturity to the soft-landscaping scheme. A new shopping centre close to where I live planted a lot of small native and naturalized shrubs in its general scheme and car park, but then included a few large palm trees inside its main entrance. The designers made a choice of effect versus cost, and you need to do the same.

Ajuga reptans 'Braunherz'

The most important thing to avoid when purchasing a container-grown plant is a pot-bound plant. These are fairly easy to spot: they tend to have weeds and moss growing on top of the compost and there are likely to be roots growing out of the drainage holes. In really bad cases the plant will be well attached to the gravel below the pot, bringing some up with it when you try to lift it. If neither of these characteristics is present and you are still not sure, try to tap the pot off the plant. It should come away with ease. If you can see hardly any of the compost and roots twining around and around, avoid that plant. It could be saved, with a bit of tender, loving care, but will probably never perform as well as a 'fresh' plant. Ideally the roots should look something like the one shown in the photograph below, with nice white growing tips. If you can see a few of these growing tips sticking out of the drainage holes, it is probably ideal for planting, so buy it.

This plant is not pot-bound

A bare-root plant is precisely what it says, a plant whose roots are not in compost or protected by a pot – they are bare. They also may be referred to as '**field-grown**'. You may also come across the term '**root-wrapped**'. Hessian sacking is what is usually used to wrap the roots, but some nurseries use plastic sheeting or even a plastic pot filled with loose compost. You will distinguish the latter from container-grown plants because the pots will be covered with netting and there is likely to be a lid of some description preventing the loose compost from falling out. Obviously, you have to trust the retailer when buying root-wrapped plants, and not many nurseries will let you inspect bare-root plants before they are packed. This is because they are geared up for the mail-order trade and their work areas are not insured for public access. As with most shopping, reputable firms are the safest.

One last point on your plant purchases: if you want quick cover, plant more plants than you need in a particular space, and then remove some as they mature. This method works best with a grouping of the same type of plant, because you can then remove the weakest specimens as needed, but it is possible to do this with a mix of different plants. If you mix plants, you need to be aware of growth rates, because fast-growing plants, especially spreading ones, may swamp slower ones. This can, of course, be controlled with pruning if you enjoy the extra work. A good mix that gives a spread of interest through the year is *Rosa* 'Surrey' and *Euonymus* 'Emerald Gaiety'. The former flowers all summer, the latter is evergreen and hides the uninteresting bare branches of the rose throughout winter.

Phlomis italica, *Fuchsia magellanica* var. *gracilis* 'Aurea' and *Stipa arundinacea* planted together

Planting and Aftercare

Planting

Having selected your plants correctly, there are three factors for successful planting:

1 Water the plant thoroughly before planting
2 Keep root damage to a minimum
3 Keep the plant well watered for the first growing season (spring and summer, and autumn if it is dry)

A common mistake that some people make is to water 'little and often'. It is far, far better to drench the plant thoroughly from time to time than pour a few cupfuls on it every day. This is because water at the surface of the soil evaporates before the plants can use it and a small amount of water will never penetrate to the roots. If you are not sure, push your finger in, dig if necessary, down about 30–45mm (1–1½in); if the soil is moist there, you do not need to water. A hose pipe left trickling on the surface, or a few cans of water poured on slowly with a chance to soak in between each one are the best methods. By 'can', I mean a watering can with a rose to spread the force of the deluge; it is possible to pour a bucket of water on the garden without blasting soil everywhere, but it's hard work! A common misconception is that you don't need to water new plants that like dry conditions. They do still need watering when new. The reason that these plants can tolerate dry conditions is that they grow lots of roots, usually going deep into the ground to find water, and they obviously need time to do this. This is the time they take to become properly established.

Root damage

Keeping root damage to a minimum is not difficult with container-grown plants, unless they are pot-bound. If the plant is pot-bound, you may well need to damage the roots for the long term health of the plant, by teasing out the spiralled roots, or even by cutting the roots which will force it to grow new ones. However, the plant needs to be in a poor state for this drastic action. The vast majority of container plants will not need such attention and if you are unsure, the roots are best left alone.

Roots and oxygen

The other important factor for the roots is the amount of oxygen they receive. The roots of a plant need to breathe. If the soil is packed hard around the plant, or if it is planted too deep, at least some of the roots will die and this will affect the performance of the plant. Most plants will usually recover from this kind of damage, but they will take longer to have the desired effect in your garden and need more watering in their early years. You should always plant a container-grown plant so that the surface of the soil that was in the pot is just covered. It is hard to advise on how much you should pack the soil around the new plant, because there are many factors which affect its ability to be compacted, the most important being the type of soil. The general rule is apply your body weight with your foot (no bouncing!), or with your fingers if it is a smaller plant. You should leave the soil slightly higher than you want it to be, because it will naturally settle over the next few weeks. The soil you use to back fill the hole should contain additional quantities of organic matter (about 25 per cent) over and above any soil improvement you have already carried out. For an average-sized shrub, you should also mix in about two to three handfuls of bonemeal.

Water before you plant

As you may know from cooking and washing, a damp item is a lot easier to get wet than a dry item. With the latter, the water may run off rather than soak in. The same is true of a dry plant, so making sure it is wet before it goes in the ground means it is easier for the plant to make contact with the water around it in the soil. What also assists here is to loosen the soil at the bottom of the hole and to mix in some organic matter. For an average-sized shrub, you should also sprinkle a handful of bonemeal over the bottom and side of the hole.

Planting bulbs

When you are planting a tree or shrub, this is a good time to put in any bulbs you wish to grow underneath them. The bulbs will benefit from the water you give the tree or shrub and if you plant them later there is always the chance that you will damage the shrub's roots in the process. When you have partially filled the hole around the shrub, put in the bulbs and bury them. A simple rule for bulbs is to plant them at a depth that is equal to double their size. A bulb that is 45mm (1¾in) high needs a hole that is at least 90mm (3in) deep. As always though, there are the odd exceptions and you should read the advice on the packet if there is one.

Crocuses planted beneath a fruit tree

Aftercare

Water and mulching

At first, the most important thing that the newly planted plant needs, until it is established, is water. Mulching assists here. Old woodlands have a wonderful, rich soil. This is because, over the years, the leaves have dropped and rotted into the soil. Regular mulching in the garden imitates this woodland process, especially if you use organic material such as bark, cocoa shell or garden compost. You can even use newspapers, although you may wish to hide them under a thin layer of bark. Newspapers need to be held down in some way: a 10mm (⅜in) layer of gravel works on heavy soils, because you can fork in the gravel when the newspaper has rotted and repeat the process. The gravel is worked into the soil and improves the drainage and the result, with the rotted newspapers, is fine-quality soil.

Fertilizer

As a rule, established plants do not need fertilizer, but as with most things in life, the more you put in, the more you get out. You will find that you get more flowers, healthier plants and certainly more growth if you use a proprietary fertilizer. If you want to keep it simple, just use a general one for the whole garden. Common brands are Miracle-Gro, Phostrogen and Vitax Q4. If you wish to be organic, use fish, blood and bone in the spring and early summer with liberal top-ups of organic matter. A useful recent addition to the market is pelleted manures, which give many of the benefits of organic matter without the bulk. As organic matter, they are not really a fertilizer, although they are often sold as such, but they are a superb extra to your fertilizing regime. You will notice the difference.

Pruning, pests and diseases

Pruning and plant health problems are subjects too large to deal with here in great depth but, if you have chosen your plants correctly, you should not have too many problems. The main point of pruning is to keep the plant as you want it, particularly its size. The general rule is that you should prune after flowering, but always seek advice if you are unsure. The majority of roses are a good exception: they should be pruned hard in winter. It is usually beneficial to prune out any dead wood in a plant too.

The main plant health problems are pests and diseases. If the damage is minor, I would recommend you live with it, but there are many chemicals available to assist the modern gardener. If you are not keen on using them, diseases can be pruned out of a plant and pests can be controlled by cultural methods. Look for books on organic gardening for further advice. These books tend to concentrate on growing fruit and vegetables, but generally the advice applies to ornamental plants also. Your local garden centre will be able to advise you if you take them a piece of the damaged plant.

Camellia japonica showing 'yellows' disease

Other knocks

Plants can also sustain physical damage, inflicted by children and animals, frosts and nutrient deficiencies. The latter are unusual on ornamental plants and are often mistaken for a pest or disease. Regular applications of organic matter or fertilizers that contain trace elements will prevent these problems. Hardy plants will normally recover from frost damage without further help, though they may look a little unsightly for a while. You could remove the damaged leaves if you wish; this is particularly pertinent to evergreen plants. The same applies with broken branches, except that you should remove them by pruning just below the break. You should never prune back a branch flush to the larger branch or trunk it comes out of; always leave a small stump. This will help to prevent disease taking hold.

Pruning out frost damage on a pieris

Dead wood should be removed, because fungi that break down the branches or twigs can sometimes penetrate the living tissue, especially if the plant is already unhealthy. If any wood is diseased when you prune it out, remember to wash your secateurs afterwards and either burn the wood, or bin small quantities.

By growing the correct plants for the conditions in your garden, and by looking after the soil, you should be able to avoid this remedial work. Then you can sit back, relax and enjoy the fruits of your labours.

PLANTS THAT SPAN THE SEASONS

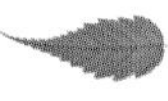

Plants that Span the Seasons

Here is a selection of plants that will provide a feature for more than one season or for a long period each year. For example, the potentilla listed does not have any particular autumn colour; it is unremarkable in winter and spring; but it will flower reliably all summer long. The list presented here is biased towards plants for the smaller garden, because of modern housing trends, but some larger plants are included.

Also, in keeping with the theme of this book, all these plants are easy to grow, as long as you plant them in the right place. None is invasive, needs regular pruning or suffers from serious pests and diseases.

All sizes quoted are for guidance only, and you should bear in mind that some plants will take a while to get to their ultimate size, particularly if conditions are not ideal.

Abies koreana (Korean fir)

TYPE: Evergreen conifer
HEIGHT: 10m (33ft)
SPREAD: 5m (16½ft)
SEASONS OF INTEREST: cones late summer onwards
CONDITIONS REQUIRED: light shade and moist soil

This conifer has excellent foliage and shape, but the main reason it is grown in gardens is for its blue cones. It starts flowering, somewhat insignificantly, in spring, and the cones can appear at a very early age for a conifer – on plants as small as 1m (3¼ft) high. It will grow best on an acid soil and not at all on very alkaline soils (greater than 7.5 pH). The needles of abies are softer than those of junipers, piceas and so on, and this makes them more pleasant to work with.

IF YOU LIKE THIS PLANT, LOOK ALSO AT...
Other abies. *Abies lasiocarpa* has some interesting garden forms; *A. procera* has superb, blue foliage and *A. balsamea* is an interesting, dwarf-growing conifer. Other conifers that may provide something similar are juniper (many garden forms and species), picea, which has many garden forms, particularly the excellent *P. omorika,* and tsuga which also comes in many different garden forms and species.

Acer griseum (paperbark maple)

TYPE: Deciduous tree
HEIGHT: 10m (33ft)
SPREAD: 8m (26ft)
SEASONS OF INTEREST: Autumn colour and winter bark
CONDITIONS REQUIRED: Likes full sun, but can tolerate light shade. Needs well-drained soil and lots of organic matter. The soil must not be soggy in winter.

The foliage of *Acer griseum* is a pleasant, light green, but this slow-growing tree is really grown for its winter bark. The new growth in spring is also attractive. It could happily be grown where the bark can be caressed by a passing admirer, such as beside a path and this would give the bark an extremely polished look. You will, however, lose the 'peeling paper' effect.

IF YOU LIKE THIS PLANT, LOOK ALSO AT... Most of the other acers. *Acer palmatum* and *A. japonicum* are large shrubs or small trees. They have more interesting foliage, but not such good bark. *Acer davidii* is one of the snake-bark maples (striped appearence), as are *A. capillipes*, *A. rufinerve* and *A. pensylvanicum*. If you like the idea of peeling bark on a shrub, investigate *Physocarpus opulifolius*.

Acer negundo 'Flamingo' (box elder)

TYPE: Deciduous tree/large shrub
HEIGHT: 4m (13ft)
SPREAD: 2m (6½ft)
SEASONS OF INTEREST: Interesting foliage all year round
CONDITIONS REQUIRED: Prefers full sun, but will tolerate light shade. Needs well-drained soil and lots of organic matter. The soil must not be soggy in winter.

This variety of *Acer negundo* is more useful than the species for the modern gardener because it is small and the new foliage in spring is more definitely coloured. The variegated foliage provides interest throughout the summer and makes a good backdrop for smaller plants. You can plant crocus or snowdrops underneath it to provide another season of interest. You could even try to match or contrast a late-spring flower with the pink of the new growth.

IF YOU LIKE THIS PLANT, LOOK ALSO AT…
Acer davidii, although this is a tree rather than a shrub, and other *A. negundo* varieties. *Acer palmatum* and *A. japonicum* varieties also have excellent variegation. The true elders (sambucus) are less attractive, in my opinion, but they grow in a wider range of conditions, and are generally easier to grow.

Acer palmatum 'Dissectum' (Japanese maple)

TYPE: Deciduous shrub
HEIGHT AND SPREAD: 6–7m (19½–23ft) rounded mound (eventually), but can be kept smaller
SEASONS OF INTEREST: Strictly an autumn plant, admired for its vivid red leaves before they drop, but as with most Japanese maples, its shape and leaf form in summer are also very pleasant. Their lacy branch-work in winter can be appealing, too.
CONDITIONS REQUIRED: Does not like to be wet, particularly in winter. Lots of organic matter is recommended.

Japanese maples are shallow-rooting, so mulching is highly recommended. Although they do not like to be wet, neither are they drought-tolerant plants and mulching helps to keep a consistent level of moisture. For best results, light shade is recommended, because most Japanese maples will suffer leaf scorch in full sun. They are very good for growing in pots and can be kept smaller this way.

The Japanese maples are an excellent group of plants to consider planting bulbs, for a display of flowers before the new leaves appear in the spring. Crocus and early-flowering narcissus (daffodils) are especially recommended.

IF YOU LIKE THIS PLANT, LOOK ALSO AT...
Any of the other Japanese maples, such as *Acer palmatum* and *A. japonicum* and their varieties. You may also like some of the hebes for their rounded form, but they are otherwise quite different. Some acers are worth looking at if you have room for a tree or two; they vary from small (6–8m (19½–26ft)) to normal-sized trees such as *Acer pseudoplatanus* (sycamore). *Acer platanoides* and its varieties are worth considering, and *A. griseum* (see page 26) has the best peeling bark of any tree.

Amelanchier lamarckii

TYPE: Deciduous shrub
HEIGHT: 6m (19½ft)
SPREAD: 3m (10ft)
SEASONS OF INTEREST: White flowers and bronze-coloured new foliage in spring, and autumn colour in the form of crimson berries
CONDITIONS REQUIRED: Prefers full sun, and soil with a high level of organic matter

This versatile shrub can be kept small with pruning, but it is best left alone to reach its majestic maturity. It is easy to grow. The new bronze-coloured foliage in spring contrasts well with the white flowers. You can plant snowdrops or crocus underneath it to provide another season of interest. The berries are not so significant, but they do make the shrub attractive in the autumn.

IF YOU LIKE THIS PLANT, LOOK ALSO AT... Forsythia, a large, spring-flowering shrub, although it provides little of note for the rest of the year. If you have an acid soil, try deciduous azaleas. The Japanese maples – *Acer palmatum* (see pages 11 and 28–29) and *A. japonicum* – give good autumn colour. Other plants that would fulfil a similar niche in the garden are the deciduous viburnums, such as *Viburnum plicatum*, magnolias and the larger cotoneasters, such as *C. frigidus* 'Cornubia'. Consider crab-apple tree varieties (malus) as well.

Berberis × *carminea* 'Buccaneer' (berberis)

TYPE: Deciduous shrub
HEIGHT: 1.5m (5ft)
SPREAD: 1.2m (4ft)
SEASONS OF INTEREST: Autumn leaf colour and berries; flowers in late spring
CONDITIONS REQUIRED: Likes full sun

This outstanding plant is rarely seen, overshadowed by some of its common brethren which are often used in parks and gardens. However, it has the best autumn coloration of any berberis, and has better fruiting than most. There are other x *carminea* varieties: 'Pirate King' is more generally available than most and is an excellent plant.

IF YOU LIKE THIS PLANT, LOOK ALSO AT...
Other deciduous berberis. *Berberis* × *ottawensis* 'Superba' has purple leaves and excellent flowers; *B. thunbergii* has a large range of garden varieties, such as *B. thunbergii* 'Rose Glow', an excellent variegated purple form; and *B. wilsonae* has good berrying. For evergreen berberis, see the entry for *Berberis darwinii* on page 32. For other autumn colour or berrying plants, see the lists on pages 95 and 99.

Berberis darwinii (berberis, barberry)

TYPE: Evergreen shrub
HEIGHT: 50cm (20in)
SPREAD: 1.2m (4ft)
SEASONS OF INTEREST: Spring flowers and autumn berries
CONDITIONS REQUIRED: Likes full sun and moist soil

The best way to give this plant the moist soil it prefers is with a high level of organic matter. It will grow in light shade, but it will not flower as well as in full sun. The orange flowers cover the plant in late spring; the deep blue berries in autumn are less obvious. As with all berberis, it has thorns.

IF YOU LIKE THIS PLANT, LOOK ALSO AT...
Other evergreen berberis, such as *Berberis × stenophylla*, *B. verruculosa*, *B. julianae*, *B. candidula* and *B. linearifolia*, are of particular note. The deciduous berberis may also be of interest. Other small, evergreen shrubs include hebe, *Viburnum davidii*, pyracantha varieties, escallonia and ceanothus varieties. See the list of plants that give berries, on page 99, if that is the feature you require.

Chaenomeles × *superba* 'Rowallane' (ornamental quince)

TYPE: Deciduous shrub
HEIGHT: 1m (3¼ft)
SPREAD: 2m (6½ft)
SEASONS OF INTEREST: Spring flowers; leaves in summer; fruits in summer/autumn
CONDITIONS REQUIRED: Full sun and good drainage

This shrub can be rather open in habit, but it needs the space for its profusion of flowers and fruit. The latter are edible, normally being used to make quince jelly. On poor soils it will need regular feeding. A generous amount of organic matter will assist with this.

IF YOU LIKE THIS PLANT, LOOK ALSO AT... The many other chaenomeles, which come in various sizes and flower colours. Forsythia also offers a dramatic spring display. Some of the shrub roses have a similar appearance to chaenomeles in their branch arrangement; *Rosa* 'Fruhlingsgold' for example. Amelanchier (page 30) may also appeal.

Choisya ternata (Mexican orange blossom)

TYPE: Evergreen shrub
HEIGHT: 2m (6½ft)
SPREAD: 2m (6½ft)
SEASONS OF INTEREST: White flowers in late spring; interesting form all year
CONDITIONS REQUIRED: Full sun or light shade

Choisya is a deservedly popular garden plant, because it is easy to grow and it has very good foliage and shape. It will grow in most soils, but it does not like to be wet in the winter. Plant it near a path and the foliage will give off a gentle fragrance when you brush past it. The flowers are also fragrant. It can be pruned and you may need to remove the odd branch that spoils the overall shape. The golden form, *Choisya ternata* 'Sundance' is unbeatable for its colour. It flowers and reaches a similar size to the species, but it must have light shade, for the leaves will scorch in full sun.

IF YOU LIKE THIS PLANT, LOOK ALSO AT... Hebes have some species and varieties that will give a rounded form – *Hebes buxifolia*, for example – and they are all evergreen. No other plants look quite like choisya, but lupinus has similar, star-shaped leaves.

Clematis alpina

TYPE: Deciduous climber
HEIGHT: 2.5m (8ft)
SPREAD: 1.5m (5ft)
SEASONS OF INTEREST: Spring flowers; summer seed heads
CONDITIONS REQUIRED: Prefers shade (light shade for best flowering)

Although this plant will grow in most conditions, it will perform best if the roots are not in direct sun and the soil has a high level of organic matter. There are varieties available with different flowers, but they grow to the same size.

IF YOU LIKE THIS PLANT, LOOK ALSO AT... Other deciduous species of clematis, such as *Clematis orientalis* and *C. tangutica*. There are evergreen types as well, such as *Clematis armandii*, while some other clematis will develop attractive seeds (except the large-flowered hybrids such as 'Jackmanii' and 'Hagley Hybrid'). You can get clematis for flowering at any time except winter. If what you need is a shade-loving climber, then consider *Hydrangea petiolaris*. *Garrya elliptica* is also recommended for a shaded wall. It has catkins in early spring.

Cornus canadensis (creeping dogwood)

TYPE: Perennial
HEIGHT: 15cm (6in)
SPREAD: Indefinite
SEASONS OF INTEREST: Green flowers in late spring and wine-coloured autumn foliage
CONDITIONS REQUIRED: Shade (light shade for best flowering), and soil with a high level of organic matter

This plant is mysteriously unusual in gardens. In late spring it bears green flowers within white, specialized leaves, called **bracts**. Red berries often follow the wine-coloured autumn foliage. It is excellent for growing underneath trees and will tolerate dry shade. For best results, it needs moisture, hence the need for a lot of organic matter.

IF YOU LIKE THIS PLANT, LOOK ALSO AT…
Pachysandra terminalis which, although it does not flower, will grow even in the darkest shade and has interesting evergreen foliage. *Vinca major* and *V. minor* – which are evergreen and bear blue flowers – are also worth considering. The perennial geraniums, such as *Geranium sanguineum*, prefer full sun, but will tolerate light shade and do better in dry conditions. Hostas are superb foliage plants, and need light shade and moist conditions; most have blue flowers in summer/autumn.

Cornus florida rubra (flowering dogwood)

TYPE: Deciduous large shrub/small tree
HEIGHT: 6m (19½ft)
SPREAD: 8m (26ft)
SEASONS OF INTEREST: Late spring flowers and autumn leaf colour
CONDITIONS REQUIRED: Full sun and good drainage

There are quite a few varieties of *Cornus florida*, some of which are smaller growing, although they still make large shrubs. When the plant flowers, what you actually see is the colour of a specialized leaf (bract) around an insignificant flower. With *Cornus florida rubra* these are red; they vary from white to pinks in other varieties. The most common dogwoods like a moist, even wet, soil, but this is not true of this species. It still likes a high level of organic matter, however.

IF YOU LIKE THIS PLANT, LOOK ALSO AT...
Other *Cornus florida* varieties. Also *C. mas* and *C. kousa*. Some sorbus species make excellent small trees for the garden – *Sorbus cashmiriana*, for example. Malus (crab-apples) may also be worth investigation, particularly *Malus sargentii*. If you are wanting a large shrub, then consider viburnum – *Viburnum* × *carlcephalum*, for example – and magnolia, escallonia and syringa. If white flowers are suitable, *Holodiscus discolor* may be of interest.

Corokia cotoneaster (wire netting plant)

TYPE: Evergreen shrub
HEIGHT: 2m (6½ft)
SPREAD: 2.5m (8ft)
SEASONS OF INTEREST: Late spring flowers and red fruits in autumn
CONDITIONS REQUIRED: Full sun and good drainage recommended

The yellow flowers are fragrant, but this shrub is really grown for its dense mass of tiny branches, which gives it its odd common name of wire netting plant. To stay looking its best it needs shelter from the cold and wind, although it copes well with coastal conditions. It likes a high level of organic matter in the soil.

IF YOU LIKE THIS PLANT, LOOK ALSO AT...
The cotoneasters for something that fulfils a similar function (*C. horizontalis*, for example), although there is no plant quite like *Corokia cotoneaster*. Berberis may also appeal, because they bear flowers and berries and some are evergreen. Look for *Berberis verruculosa* and *B. candidula*. The deciduous berberis look similar to the corokia in winter. There are other corokia species, but they look very different.

Corylus avellana 'Contorta' (twisted/contorted hazel)

TYPE: Deciduous shrub or small tree
HEIGHT: 5m (16½ft)
SPREAD: 5m (16½ft)
SEASONS OF INTEREST: Catkins in late winter/early spring; twisted branches in winter
CONDITIONS REQUIRED: Full sun and good drainage recommended

The contorted hazel, or Harry Lauder's walking stick, is a glorious example of a plant that produces catkins. The only one with better catkins in the UK is *Garrya elliptica*, but that does not provide much interest for the rest of the year. The twisted branches of the hazel are a good winter feature. You need to watch for suckers coming from the base of the plant, recognizable from the way they grow straight, pushing up between the other branches.

IF YOU LIKE THIS PLANT, LOOK ALSO AT… *Salix matsudana* 'Tortuosa'; it does not bear catkins, but it is more dramatic in winter. *Corylus colurna*, on the other hand, has good catkins, but not very interesting branches. *Betula pendula* 'Youngii' is a small tree, but with its weeping branches it can be treated like a shrub in how it fills a space. *Betula pendula* 'Tristis' meanwhile has branches that twist slightly.

Cotoneaster horizontalis (fish bone cotoneaster)

TYPE: Deciduous shrub
HEIGHT: 1m (3¼ft)
SPREAD: 1.5m (5ft)
SEASONS OF INTEREST: White/pale pink flowers in spring; red berries in autumn
CONDITIONS REQUIRED: Sun or light shade. Any soil, except that it doesn't like to be wet in winter

Cotoneaster horizontalis is easy to grow and is deservedly popular in British gardens, but this does not mean we should take it for granted. A good specimen is a splendid sight. If trained against a wall, it can grow taller than the height given here. This is often done, because it is an excellent way to show off the distinctive branchwork. A high level of organic matter will help wherever you live, but full sun and good drainage will give the best results.

IF YOU LIKE THIS PLANT, LOOK ALSO AT...
...the other cotoneasters, because this is a huge genus of evergreen and deciduous plants. All the smaller shrubs, such as *Cotoneaster adpressus* and *C. microphyllus*, are worth investigation. Closest to *Cotoneaster horizontalis* in general appearance are probably the pyracanthas, which also flower and berry. They do tend to be larger shrubs than most cotoneasters, but newer, smaller varieties, such as *Pyracanthus coccinea* 'Red Cushion', are appearing all the time.

Crocus 'Cream Beauty' (crocus)

TYPE: Bulb
HEIGHT: 10cm (4in)
SPREAD: 3cm (1¼in)
SEASONS OF INTEREST: Flowers and fragrance in early spring
CONDITIONS REQUIRED: A good level of organic matter and good drainage

This particular crocus was selected for its fragrant flowers. There are hundreds of different crocus species and varieties and all are worth growing, especially as they do not take up much room. They can be naturalized in a lawn, and they can be mown over earlier in the summer than narcissus – a fact which may appeal to some gardeners. They do well under deciduous trees and shrubs, where they can extend the period of interest in that part of the garden.

IF YOU LIKE THIS PLANT, LOOK ALSO AT...
Other crocus and there are hundreds of different galanthus and narcissus. Chionodoxa may also be of interest, as might anemone, puschkinia or muscari. It will depend on what you are trying to achieve in the garden and the conditions that prevail. Chionodoxa is the closest to crocus in terms of the niche it fills.

Cryptomeria japonica 'Elegans' (cryptomeria, Japanese cedar)

TYPE: Evergreen conifer
HEIGHT: 3m (10ft)
SPREAD: 1.2m (4ft)
SEASONS OF INTEREST: Fascinating foliage all year round; autumn/winter colour
CONDITIONS REQUIRED: Full sun and good drainage

This plant prefers a lime-free (i.e. acid) soil, but it will grow in most soils if provided with a good amount of organic matter. It will grow well in light shade. The feathery foliage makes an excellent backdrop for other plants. It is a plant that is best left untrimmed, but you may find that the bottom branches die as it ages, particularly if it occupies a shaded position. I have seen it with clematis and tropaeolum growing through it to provide summer colour. This was very effective, though you need to be careful what colour flower you select.

IF YOU LIKE THIS PLANT, LOOK ALSO AT... The other *Cryptomeria japonica* varieties. Most are more bushy than upright. *Cryptomeria japonica* 'Spiralis' has excellent foliage. Chamaecyparis and thuja both have soft foliage, but not as fine as cryptomeria.

Dicentra spectabilis
(bleeding heart)

TYPE: Perennial
HEIGHT: 1m (3¼ft)
SPREAD: 60cm (24in)
SEASONS OF INTEREST: Flowers in late spring and early summer
CONDITIONS REQUIRED: Light shade and good drainage

To be honest, this popular plant only really has one major feature time – the spring – but I think that its foliage and habit make it worth having in any garden. It is easy to grow, and will perform better with a good level of organic matter in the soil. If grown in full sun, it may get leaf scorch and tend to look rather anaemic.

IF YOU LIKE THIS PLANT, LOOK ALSO AT… The other varieties of this plant. 'Alba', a white form, is striking, but the species is still the best plant overall. There are other dicentras, but none as elegant as *Dicentra spectabilis*. *Dicentra formosa* is quite different but highly recommended. Other perennials with good foliage are astilbes, heuchera, hosta, paeonia and some geraniums. Of these, astilbes and hostas prefer moist conditions.

Elaeagnus pungens 'Maculata' (elaeagnus)

TYPE: Evergreen shrub
HEIGHT: 3m (10ft)
SPREAD: 4m (13ft)
SEASONS OF INTEREST: Variegated foliage all year round
CONDITIONS REQUIRED: Full sun or light shade and good drainage

This shrub is grown for its foliage, but it does bear flowers, albeit insignificant ones, in the autumn, and they are fragrant. It will grow in any soil, but does not like to be wet in winter. You may occasionally get a branch with leaves that are all green, which should be removed to keep the plant variegated.

IF YOU LIKE THIS PLANT, LOOK ALSO AT...
Other good elaeagnus: *Elaeagnus* × *ebbingei* and its varieties are very good. *Elaeagnus* × *ebbingei* 'Limelight' is a superb plant with similar variegation and size to *E. pungens* 'Maculata', but with a faster growth rate. Other evergreen shrubs of note are escallonia (for their flowers), ilex (for their variegation, flowers and berries), euonymus (for their foliage), and pieris (for their spring flowers) if you have an acid soil. Most common plants are available in a variegated form if that is the feature that appeals to you.

Erica × *darleyensis* (heather)

TYPE: Evergreen shrub
HEIGHT: 45cm (18in)
SPREAD: 1m (3¼ft)
SEASONS OF INTEREST: Late winter/early spring flowers and good foliage all year round
CONDITIONS REQUIRED: Prefers full sun, but light shade is fine

All ericas like a soil with a high level of organic matter. This species, and *Erica carnea*, are lime-tolerant so they can be grown in any soil; all other heathers need an acid soil. Although it has not been bred as much as *Erica carnea*, there are many varieties of *E.* × *darleyensis*, offering different flower colours and heights.

IF YOU LIKE THIS PLANT, LOOK ALSO AT… *Erica carnea* and its varieties. If you have an acid soil, any other erica will be suitable, as will the other heathers – calluna and daboecia – though these two plants are only summer-flowering. You can get an *Erica carnea* variety that will flower for any time of the year. Many have foliage that provides interest all year round.

Fothergilla gardenii
(witch alder)

TYPE: Deciduous shrub
HEIGHT: 1m (3¼ft)
SPREAD: 1m (3¼ft)
SEASONS OF INTEREST: White flowers in late spring and red autumn foliage
CONDITIONS REQUIRED: Acid soil and full sun for best performance

All fothergillas like a lot of organic matter in the soil. They will do well in all but heavy shade, but the autumn colour is most dramatic if they are provided with full sun. The 'bottlebrush' flowers appear before the leaves and so they are the first signs of life on this plant each year. Fothergillas will leaf after most other plants in the garden, so do not worry if they do not look alive in early spring.

IF YOU LIKE THIS PLANT, LOOK ALSO AT...
Fothergilla major, which is very similar, but larger. Deciduous azaleas are worth investigating for their spring flowers and autumn colour on acid soil. Corylopsis are also interesting. Eucryphia or halesia (silver bell, snowdrop tree) may fit the bill if you want something larger.

Fuchsia magellanica (fuchsia, lady's eardrop)

TYPE: Deciduous shrub
HEIGHT: 2m (6½ft)
SPREAD: 2m (6½ft)
SEASONS OF INTEREST: Flowers in the summer and autumn
CONDITIONS REQUIRED: Full sun or light shade and good drainage

This fuchsia is one of the largest in the genus and is often seen as hedging in milder climates like those enjoyed by Cornwall and the Isle of Man, among others. It is fully hardy, but does not like a wet soil in winter. It's extended flowering season make this plant a worthy candidate for this book. It will usually start to flower in early to mid-summer and go right through until after the first frosts. In a mild autumn this can mean four or five months of colour.

IF YOU LIKE THIS PLANT, LOOK ALSO AT...
The thousands of other fuchsias; make sure you choose a hardy variety if you intend to leave it in the garden. *Fuchsia* 'Tom Thumb' is a good, small-growing variety; *F.* 'Mrs Popple' is probably the most well-known hardy fuchsia and *F.* 'Riccartonii' is an excellent, large shrub fuchsia.

Galanthus nivalis (snowdrop)

TYPE: Bulb
HEIGHT: 60cm (24in)
SPREAD: 10cm (4in)
SEASONS OF INTEREST: Late winter/early spring flowers
CONDITIONS REQUIRED: Shade and moist soil

Although snowdrops like a moist soil, they will rot if they get too wet in the autumn and winter. Therefore, the best way to keep them successfully is to have a soil with a high level of organic matter. They have been bred extensively, but they all bear white flowers. The detail of variations on some of the flowers can be exquisite. Although this plant does not quite fit within the remit of this book, as it only gives one season, it performs an important role of extending the season of interest in a particular area when planted beneath trees and shrubs. To me snowdrops are one of the true heralds of spring, even if they are poking out of the snow.

IF YOU LIKE THIS PLANT, LOOK ALSO AT...
Crocus for planting beneath shrubs, the only other option for very early flowers. Narcissus are good, but they flower a little later. If what you need is a yellow flower in winter, then try *Eranthis hyemalis* (winter aconite).

Genista lydia

TYPE: Evergreen shrub
HEIGHT: 60cm (24in)
SPREAD: 60cm (24in)
SEASONS OF INTEREST: Late May/June
CONDITIONS REQUIRED: A sunny position in well-drained soil

Genista lydia is really a single-season plant, but the blaze of colour on established bushes is spectacular and contributes to it being one of my favourite plants. It is not devoid of purpose the rest of the year, however; it is evergreen and forms a rounded hummock which lends structure to the garden in winter. The foliage is most unusual in that there are no recognizable leaves; all the shoots and branches are green instead. It is a pale green, and so contrasts well with dark purple plants, among others.

Genista and cytisus form the two genera that make up the group commonly known as 'brooms'. Brooms do not like a soggy soil in winter because their roots tend to rot. In a well-drained soil, however, they can live with low levels of light, but they all perform much better in full sun.

IF YOU LIKE THIS PLANT, ALSO LOOK AT...
Genista hispanica, a slightly smaller, prickly version of *G. lydia*; hebes, particularly the small-leafed varieties; and most cytisus varieties, although many will get much larger than *G. lydia*.

Hebe cuppressoides (hebe)

TYPE: Evergreen shrub
HEIGHT: 1.2m (4ft)
SPREAD: 1.2m (4ft)
SEASONS OF INTEREST: Lilac-blue flowers in early summer and all year structure
CONDITIONS REQUIRED: Full sun and good drainage

This plant provides excellent structure in the garden all year round. It helps to break up the straight edge of patios or paths. The unusual foliage looks more like scales or needles than leaves. There are several varieties available: 'Boughton Dome' has white flowers and is much smaller, reaching a height of 30cm (12in) and spreading to 60cm (24in).

IF YOU LIKE THIS PLANT, LOOK ALSO AT...
Other varieties of hebe, although not many others make such a formal shape as *Hebes cuppressoides*. Armeria may be of interest, although it is more grass-like in appearance. The shrub potentillas often make a nice mound and generally have better flowering than hebes. It would also be worth considering some dwarf or slow-growing conifers if it is the mound shape which you find appealing.

Hedera helix 'Glacier' (ivy)

TYPE: Evergreen climber
HEIGHT: 2.5m (8ft)
SPREAD: 2m (6½ft)
SEASONS OF INTEREST: Interesting foliage all year round
CONDITIONS REQUIRED: Shade

Ivies are not fussy about soil. In fact, they have been known to grow in rubble. They do best in light shade, being self-clinging, this variety does not need a support system; most *Hedera helix* varieties are self-clinging. Ivies can also be used as ground cover and are excellent for covering garden banks, old tree stumps, and so on.

IF YOU LIKE THIS PLANT, LOOK ALSO AT...
The many other *Hedera helix* varieties: *H. helix* 'Buttercup' is an interesting golden form, but it is not self-clinging. *H. helix* 'Goldheart' is a deservedly popular variegated ivy. There are other ivies, such as *Hedera colchica* and varieties, but their leaves are bigger so they do not look as delicate as *H. helix*. The only other climbers that do not require trellises or other means of support are parthenocissus. They give superb autumn colour and have good foliage in the summer too.

Heuchera 'Plum Puddin'

TYPE: Perennial
HEIGHT: 45cm (18in)
SPREAD: 45cm (18in)
SEASONS OF INTEREST: Flowers in summer; interesting foliage all year round
CONDITIONS REQUIRED: Light shade

Heucheras like good drainage and a high level of organic matter. This particular variety is a recent introduction, but reflects the genus generally in the way it flowers. It also has interesting year-round foliage, except in colder winters. Even the varieties with plain green leaves look good. You need to remove the old flower stalks: this will keep them tidy and encourage more flowering.

IF YOU LIKE THIS PLANT, LOOK ALSO AT... Other heucheras: *Heuchera micrantha* var. *diversiflora* 'Palace Purple' is a very good purple-leafed form, with pink flowers. *Heuchera chlorantha* 'Chocolate Ruffles' is another with interestingly marked foliage. Other perennials with flowers on stalks above the foliage are saxifrage, hosta, primula, pulmonaria and epimedium. All but the epimedium like the same conditions as heuchera. If you have a sunny spot, you may wish to consider lavandula (lavenders); they are shrubs, but they provide interesting foliage, with the added bonus of excellent summer flowering and a wonderful fragrance that you can harvest.

Hydrangea petiolaris (climbing hydrangea)

TYPE: Deciduous climber
HEIGHT AND SPREAD: Up to 15m (49ft)
SEASONS OF INTEREST: May/June flowering; winter branch work
CONDITIONS REQUIRED: Soil with a high level of organic matter

Hydrangea petiolaris is not fussy about light levels, although it is traditionally used as a deep-shade, flowering climber. It is especially good for north-facing walls, is deciduous, and though does not give good autumn colour, it does have interesting bark which makes it useful to have around in winter. The buds in early spring are also quite prominent.

A good way to extend the flowering season is to grow a clematis with the hydrangea, letting the branches intertwine. You need to choose your clematis with care, because some flower in May/June as well. These are mostly the large-flowered hybrids. Go for a species clematis, such as *Clematis alpina* or *C. tangutica*, or a variety like 'Ville de Lyon', 'The President' or 'Jackmanii'.

IF YOU LIKE THIS PLANT, LOOK ALSO AT...
If you are looking for a self-clinging climber, look at ivies or some of the species clematis; no other plant is quite like *Hydrangea petiolaris*. If you have light shade and want flowers, look at clematis or roses.

Juniperus squamata 'Blue Star' (juniper)

TYPE: Evergreen conifer
HEIGHT: 60cm (24in)
SPREAD: 1m (3¼ft)
SEASONS OF INTEREST: All year round blue foliage and interesting form
CONDITIONS REQUIRED: Full sun and good drainage recommended

This superb blue-coloured plant will tolerate light shade but not wet soils. It grows into an irregular mound which contrasts well with many other plants. I have seen it used to cover an area of bankside, with clematis growing through it quite effectively.

IF YOU LIKE THIS PLANT, LOOK ALSO AT... *Juniperus squamata* 'Blue Carpet' – a similar colour, but prostrate. *Juniperus squamata* 'Meyeri' is also blue, but will grow to 5m (16½ft) high and wide. There are thousands of other garden varieties of juniper and if none of those is suitable, then chamaecyparis, tsuga, thuja and cryptomeria may be worth investigating. *Cedrus atlantica* var. *glauca* is a tree with blue foliage. *Pyrus salicifolia* 'Pendula' is an excellent large shrub or small tree. Artemisia is a genus of perennials renowned for their blue-grey foliage. Any plant with *glauca* in the name will have blue foliage in some form.

Kolkwitzia amabilis 'Pink Cloud' (beauty bush)

TYPE: Deciduous shrub
HEIGHT: 3m (10ft)
SPREAD: 3m (10ft)
SEASONS OF INTEREST: Pink flowers late spring/early summer; foliage colour in autumn
CONDITIONS REQUIRED: Full sun and good drainage

This shrub is an amazing sight when in flower, because the whole plant is covered with the pink flowers. It is best left unpruned except to remove dead wood. This is because the branches arch upwards to form the fountain-shaped mature bush; it is very hard to prune this shape effectively without making it look messy. It needs soil with a plenty of organic matter.

IF YOU LIKE THIS PLANT, LOOK ALSO AT... Abelia species and varieties, which bear flowers but won't give you the autumn colour. Lilacs and syringa (species and varieties) also bear attractive flowers and are fairly easy to grow. They do not like acid soils, however. *Cotinus coggygria* and its varieties will give you both summer flowers and autumn colour on a large shrub.

Lamium maculatum 'Beacon Silver' (dead nettle)

TYPE: Perennial
HEIGHT: 20cm (8in)
SPREAD: 1m (3¼ft)
SEASONS OF INTEREST: Summer flowers
CONDITIONS REQUIRED: Light shade and moist soil

This plant, although perennial, will often keep its leaves right through the winter. It will lose them in a hard winter, or in an extended period of drought, from which it may recover. A high level of organic matter in the soil will reduce problems during dry weather, as will mulching. It must not be sited in full sun, or the leaves will scorch. There are many varieties of *Lamium maculatum*, grown mostly for their different kinds of foliage, but also for the colour of their flowers.

IF YOU LIKE THIS PLANT, LOOK ALSO AT... Other lamiums. Hostas, trilliums, primula, astilbes and convallaria (lily of the valley) also like the same conditions. Other mat-forming or carpeting perennials are geraniums, pulmonaria, mentha, *Galium odoratum* and mimulus varieties.

Lythrum salicaria (purple loosestrife)

TYPE: Perennial
HEIGHT: 120–150cm (4-5ft), though occasionally taller
SPREAD: Forms clump approx. 45cm (18in) diameter
SEASONS OF INTEREST: Flowers June to September; good autumn colour
CONDITIONS REQUIRED: A good soil and any level of light except heavy shade

Lythrum salicaria is native to the United Kingdom and has been hybridized. The most common variety is 'Firecandle', with redder flowers, which grows to a height of about 100cm (40in). The foliage turns bright red as it dies in autumn.

Moisture is vital for good results and lythrum will even grow in a bog garden. If your soil does not retain moisture, use lots of organic matter before planting and mulch diligently. Indeed, mulching is recommended in all but pond situations. If the plant gets too dry, it will cease flowering and have autumn early, but it should return next year as normal.

IF YOU LIKE THIS PLANT, LOOK ALSO AT...
Lythrum virgatum and its varieties, which are slightly daintier and shorter – around 60cm (24in) – but which require the same conditions. *Polemonium caeruleum* does not grow as tall as the lythrums, but is a similar type of perennial.

Miscanthus sinensis 'Zebrinus'

TYPE: Perennial
HEIGHT: 1.5m (5ft)
SPREAD: 45cm (18in)
SEASONS OF INTEREST: Summer foliage and autumn seed heads (some years)
CONDITIONS REQUIRED: Full sun and good drainage

This plant is most unusual in that the variegations are horizontal, across the leaf, rather than vertical. It forms a grass-like clump which can look very effective next to paving, gravel or water. It also makes a good contrast with plants whose leaves are more conventional. I have planted some of the taller-growing narcissus under 'Zebrinus' so that the flowers came up out of its foliage.

IF YOU LIKE THIS PLANT, LOOK ALSO AT...
The other miscanthus; although none has this variegation, they are still interesting *Hakonechloa macra* 'Aureola' will give a similar effect and there are many other golden grasses, *Carex morrowii* 'Evergold', for example. If you have a damp location, *Scirpus tabernaemontani* 'Zebrinus' also has horizontal variegation and will even grow in ponds. Bamboos may also be worth trying; see *Nandina domestica* 'Firepower' opposite.

Nandina domestica 'Firepower' (sacred bamboo)

TYPE: Evergreen shrub
HEIGHT: 1m (3¼ft)
SPREAD: 75cm (30in)
SEASONS OF INTEREST: Interesting foliage all year round; autumn/winter leaf colour
CONDITIONS REQUIRED: Full sun, moist soil with a high level of organic matter

This bamboo-like shrub may lose its leaves in harder winters, so it is best to plant it in a sheltered position. It does have small, white flowers in summer, and may have red fruits afterwards. The species is similar, but larger and not as colourful in autumn/winter.

IF YOU LIKE THIS PLANT, LOOK ALSO AT...
The actual bamboos: arundinaria, phyllostachys, chusquea, sasa and bambusa. If you are wanting plants which change colour for the winter, then many ericas (heathers) do, and so does cryptomeria. Some other conifers change as well, *Thuja occidentalis* 'Rheingold', for example. Some grasses may also be suitable. See the list of plants that bear berries, on page 99, if that is the feature which interests you.

Narcissus 'Tête-à-tête' (daffodil)

TYPE: Bulb
HEIGHT: 30cm (12in)
SPREAD: 10cm (4in)
SEASONS OF INTEREST: Early spring flowers
CONDITIONS REQUIRED: Full sun or light shade and any soil, as long as it is not wet in winter. Good for container growing

'Tete-a-tete' is an excellent example of the smaller-growing daffodils, and one of the most common. It is often found as an indoor flower, but it is fully hardy if you observe the point about not being wet in winter, as this will rot the bulb. Although it does not give more than one season, it is a good subject for planting underneath trees and shrubs to add colour to a garden early in the year. And it can also be naturalized in a lawn, as is usually done with larger varieties. Although this variety has one of the longest-lasting flowering periods, there are many other dwarf daffodils available. It is best to purchase them is in late summer/autumn, at which time they are sold in packets rather than planted in pots.

IF YOU LIKE THIS PLANT, LOOK ALSO AT...
The thousands of other narcissus varieties; the two main points to consider are the flowers (many are fragrant) and the height that they will grow to.

Nigella damascena
(love in a mist)

TYPE: Hardy annual
HEIGHT: 60cm (24in)
SPREAD: Indefinite
SEASONS OF INTEREST: Summer flowers and foliage
CONDITIONS REQUIRED: Full sun

To get the best results from this easy-to-grow plant, there should be a good level of organic matter in the soil and good drainage. It is normally available as mixed colours in seed packets, but you should be able to find single colours if that suits your garden better. Some garden centres also sell it as a bedding plant in spring, which is a good idea if you want to be more specific about where it grows in the first year. You must leave the seed heads after flowering, or collect the seed from them, if you want to have plants the following year.

IF YOU LIKE THIS PLANT, LOOK ALSO AT... Artemisia, which has similar foliage. Other hardy annuals include anchusa, calendula, centaurea (a similar flower to nigella), eschscholzia (superb flowers), lavatera (also comes as a perennial), some lupinus (can be a perennial, too), papaver (poppy) and scabiosa. There are also some biennials, one of the best examples being digitalis (foxglove).

Paeonia mascula (peony)

TYPE: Perennial
HEIGHT: 1m (3¼ft)
SPREAD: 1m (3¼ft)
SEASONS OF INTEREST: Late spring flowers, seed pods
CONDITIONS REQUIRED: Full sun, good drainage, and lots of organic matter

Most peonies found these days are hybrids; there is a huge assortment of colours, sizes and double flowers. Most are of a similar size to the plant illustrated here, but there are deciduous shrub forms, such as *Paeonia lutea*, which grow to a height of 1.5m (5ft).

IF YOU LIKE THIS PLANT, LOOK ALSO AT...
The many other peonies. For a similar, bushy form, take a look at rheum, astilbe, and some of the geraniums and lupinus. No other flowers look quite like peonies; roses are probably the closest, especially the species flowers. The vast majority of perennials like full sun, and thrive in soil with a high level of organic matter. Refer to the list of plants that like dry soils on page 108.

Phormium tenax 'Purpureum' (phormium)

TYPE: Evergreen shrub
HEIGHT: 2m (6½ft)
SPREAD: 1m (3¼ft)
SEASONS OF INTEREST: All-year-round foliage, summer flowers
CONDITIONS REQUIRED: Full sun, moist soil

Although this plant likes a moist soil, it will rot at the base if it gets too wet in winter, so it is best to have a high level of organic matter in the soil. It will do well in light shade, but the coloration of the leaves may not be as good as when in full sun. This plant may not flower in cooler summers, but the flowers can detract from the fountain of colourful leaves anyway.

IF YOU LIKE THIS PLANT, LOOK ALSO AT...
The other *Phormium tenax* varieties. 'Bronze Baby' is a much smaller, purple-leaved variety, excellent for container growing. Yucca have a similar, exotic appearance, and iris have blade-like leaves, plus superb flowering. Ophiopogon may be worth investigation if you want something smaller, or some of the ornamental grasses may fit the bill.

Polemonium caeruleum (Jacob's ladder)

TYPE: Perennial
HEIGHT: 75cm (30in)
SPREAD: 45cm (18in)
SEASONS OF INTEREST: Summer flowers, interesting foliage and autumn colour
CONDITIONS REQUIRED: Full sun and good drainage

Although strictly with its flowering, a single-season plant, Jacob's ladder provides finely divided foliage, and some colour as it dies down in the autumn. There are varieties if you want another flower colour, though they may take some searching out. 'Alba', a variety with white flowers, should be readily available.

IF YOU LIKE THIS PLANT, ALSO LOOK AT...
You might like to include *Lythrum salicaria* if conditions are moist. Other polemoniums are also available. Other perennials that may be of interest are irises (the foliage can be interesting, the flowers are outstanding, and they tolerate various soil/light conditions); stachys (foliage not as interesting, but will live in the same conditions), and *Geranium* 'Johnsons Blue' (good foliage and flowers). Also, geums and trolliuses are worth considering.

Potentilla fruticosa 'Elizabeth' (potentilla)

TYPE: Deciduous shrub
HEIGHT: 1m (3¼ft)
SPREAD: 1.5m (5ft)
SEASONS OF INTEREST: Summer to autumn flowers
CONDITIONS REQUIRED: Full sun and good drainage

Though the shrub potentillas do not really have any feature other than their flowers, they are worth a mention here because of the length of their flowering season. Virtually all will start flowering in early summer and go right through until after the first frosts. This particular variety was selected as one that can be relied upon to give a long season. However, the foliage is also of interest and, like most varieties, it grows into a nicely rounded or hummock form. A high level of organic matter is recommended.

IF YOU LIKE THIS PLANT, LOOK ALSO AT...
The other shrub potentillas, and some of the perennial potentillas if you like the flowers. Spiraea are similar in form; they will not flower as long but they will tolerate moist conditions. Ceanothuses are generally bigger, but like similar conditions. Some hebes will give similar hummock or mound forms and summer flowers.

Prunus 'Shirofugen' (flowering cherry)

TYPE: Deciduous tree
HEIGHT: 8m (26ft)
SPREAD: 10m (33ft)
SEASONS OF INTEREST: Spring flowers, summer foliage, autumn colour and winter bark
CONDITIONS REQUIRED: Full sun, and good drainage

This tree, like all the cherries, is really grown for its excellent spring flower display. However, unlike many of the others, this particular variety has superb autumn colour. It is best grown in large areas, because the dark foliage can make a small space seem more enclosed. Most cherries have interesting bark which can develop a polished look, especially if people have a habit of rubbing it.

IF YOU LIKE THIS PLANT, ALSO LOOK AT...
The hundreds of other cherries: *Prunus* 'Amanogawa' is a very upright form useful for even the smallest spaces; *P.* 'Hillierii Spire' is good for autumn colour and also grows fairly narrow; *P.* 'Kiku-shidare-zakura' is a weeping form. *P. sargentii* is slightly larger; has green foliage, but is otherwise as outstanding as 'Shirofugen' for flowering and autumn colour. You may wish to consider maluses (crab apples) too, which offer flowers in spring and fruit in autumn.

Pyracantha 'Orange Charmer' (pyracantha)

TYPE: Evergreen shrub
HEIGHT: 3m (10ft)
SPREAD: 3m (10ft)
SEASONS OF INTEREST: Late spring flowers; autumn berries
CONDITIONS REQUIRED: Good level of organic matter

This plant bears the archetypal orange pyracantha berries. There are also varieties with other shades of orange, red and yellow berries. All have white flowers and thorns. Pyracanthas will grow in any light except dense shade and they are not fussy about soil, as long as you remember the organic matter. If grown in a very cold area, or subjected to winter winds, they will lose their leaves. They grow very well against walls and fences, indeed some nurseries sell them as climbers.

IF YOU LIKE THIS PLANT, LOOK ALSO AT...
The many other forms; from low-growing, ground-cover plants, such as *P. coccinea* 'Red Cushion', to much larger plants such as *P. atalantioides,* which will grow to 5m (16½ft) high, with a spread of 4m (13ft). If you are looking for a larger, evergreen plant to provide shade, *Garrya elliptica* may be suitable. There are evergreen berberis, some of which are large shrubs; *Berberis* × *stenophylla* is one. If it is the berries you desire, see the list of berrying plants on page 99.

Pyrus calleryana 'Chanticleer' (ornamental pear)

TYPE: Deciduous tree
HEIGHT: 12m (39ft)
SPREAD: 5m (16½ft)
SEASONS OF INTEREST: Spring flowers; autumn colour
CONDITIONS REQUIRED: Full sun and good drainage

This tree is a superb sight when covered in the white flowers. It is a narrow-growing tree, so it can be considered even for quite small gardens, as long as there is space around it – this is purely for aesthetic reasons, although you should consider the future, general light level when planting any tree.

IF YOU LIKE THIS PLANT, LOOK ALSO AT... The other pyrus. Prunus and malus are also spring-flowering trees. *Magnolia kobus* or *M. stellata* and *Cornus kousa* or *C. mas* are worth investigating. If autumn colour is the desired characteristic, refer to the list of plants for autumn colour on page 95.

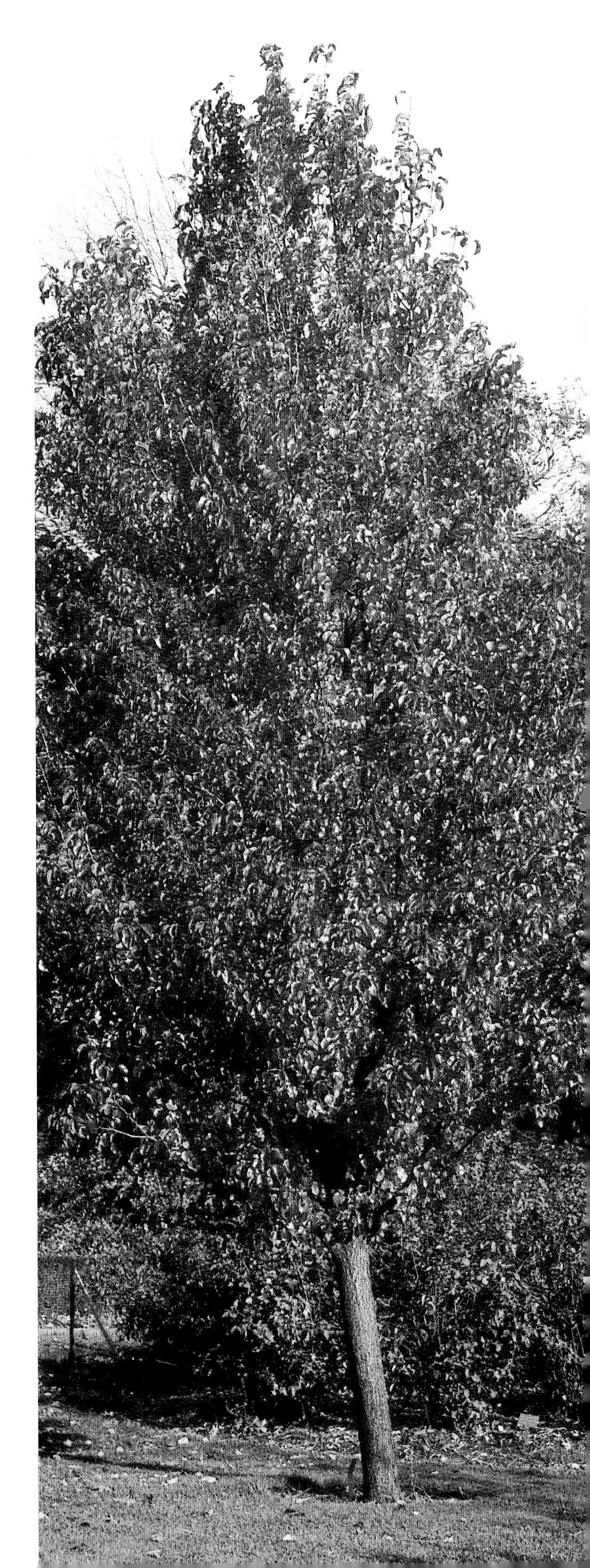

Ribes odoratum
(flowering currant, buffalo currant)

TYPE: Deciduous shrub
HEIGHT: 2m (6½ft)
SPREAD: 1.5m (5ft)
SEASONS OF INTEREST: Spring flowers; berries in summer/autumn
CONDITIONS REQUIRED: Full sun or light shade and good drainage

This plant will do best in a soil with a high level of organic matter. It is a slightly more unusual variety than is normally found in garden centres, but it is worth seeking out. Its spring display is not as good as some of the other ribes, but it fruits and has good autumn colour.

IF YOU LIKE THIS PLANT, LOOK ALSO AT...
The other ribes, particularly *Ribes sanguineum,* which has some excellent hybrids, including 'Pulborough Scarlet', which must be one of the best spring-flowering displays available. *Ribes speciosum* has fuchsia-like flowers and is highly recommended. Rubus will provide a wilder look; forsythia has glorious spring flowers and some of the deciduous viburnums bear flowers and fruit.

Rosa moyesii 'Geranium' (rose)

TYPE: Deciduous shrub
HEIGHT: 2m (6½ft)
SPREAD: 2m (6½ft)
SEASONS OF INTEREST: Summer flowers; autumn hips
CONDITIONS REQUIRED: Full sun

As with most of the species roses, this plant is not too fussy about soil, but it does not like to be wet in winter. The arching branches and clean foliage give a good effect, even before the superb flowers, which are followed shortly by the hips. *Rosa moyesii* is similar, but gets larger, and does not produce hips quite as profusely as this variety.

IF YOU LIKE THIS PLANT, LOOK ALSO AT...
Most of the species roses for they are worthy of investigation. They are much less work than the hybrids: only occasional pruning of dead wood for shaping will be required. Also, they do not have the pest and disease problems for which roses are so notorious. Another species that is particularly recommended is *Rosa rubrifolia. Rosa xanthina* 'Canarybird' and *R.* 'Dunwich Rose' are the earliest flowering. There are more roses listed on page 125.

Sorbus aucuparia 'Aspleniifolia' (rowan, mountain ash)

TYPE: Deciduous small tree
HEIGHT: 7m (23ft)
SPREAD: 5m (16½ft)
SEASONS OF INTEREST: Spring flowers; autumn berries; summer foliage
CONDITIONS REQUIRED: Full sun or light shade, and moist soil

This variety of mountain ash is very similar to the species except that it has finer, almost fern-like, foliage. The white flowers in late spring provide a good display, but the autumn berries are the real treat. Birds love them, so even the large quantity of berries produced doesn't last long. If you feed the birds regularly from a bird table, you can prolong the autumn interest of this small tree. Alternatively, provide the birds with lots of other berrying plants!

IF YOU LIKE THIS PLANT, LOOK ALSO AT...
Many other sorbuses which are just as pretty, though they do grow into large trees: *Sorbus cashmiriana* is a superb tree; *S. aria* and its varieties are also excellent. There are other *Sorbus aucuparia* varieties, including 'Fructu Luteo' which produces yellow berries; these are less popular with birds.

Spiraea × *bumalda* 'Gold Mound' (spirea)

TYPE: Deciduous shrub
HEIGHT: 50cm (20in)
SPREAD: 1m (3¼ft)
SEASONS OF INTEREST: Summer/autumn flowers
CONDITIONS REQUIRED: Full sun; prefers good drainage

Although spiraeas do not flower as long as potentillas and tend to have less interesting foliage, they are popular garden plants. This is mainly because they are cheap to buy, easy to grow and still flower for up to three months. If you choose a variety like the one shown here, the foliage can also be of interest.

IF YOU LIKE THIS PLANT, LOOK ALSO AT... The shrub-type potentillas, berberis (possibly) and it is also worth tracking down *Ceratostigma willmottianum*. Also, the smaller-growing viburnums and cotoneasters may be of interest, particularly *Viburnum opulus* 'Compactum', *Cotoneaster conspicuus* 'Decorus' and *V.* × *juddii*. If it is golden foliage that appeals, then *Choisya ternata* 'Sundance' is the premier plant, but it will get larger than this spiraea. Other golden plants include *Spiraea* × *bumalda* 'Goldflame' (also larger) and *Robinia pseudoacacia* 'Frisia' (a small tree). There are hundreds of others with golden foliage, particularly conifers; just look for *aurea* or *aureum* in the plant's name.

Taxus baccata 'Fastigiata' (yew)

TYPE: Evergreen conifer
HEIGHT: 10m (33ft)
SPREAD: 4m (13ft)
SEASONS OF INTEREST: Year-round foliage
CONDITIONS REQUIRED: Good drainage

This particular variety is much narrower growing than the species, so it is a good plant for small gardens. The upright form also provides a definite shape for the winter garden and a good backdrop for plants with a rounded form. It is slow growing after the first few years, and so its ultimate size need not be a deterrent. It will grow in full sun and all but dense shade. Yews will berry if male and female plants are present, but the seeds are toxic.

IF YOU LIKE THIS PLANT, ALSO LOOK AT...
Other *Taxus baccata* varieties, such as *T. baccata* 'Fastigiata Aurea', which is the golden form of the plant shown here; and *T. baccata* 'Repandens', which only grows 60cm (24in) high, but has a spread of up to 5m (16½ft). Other taxus may also appeal: *Taxus × media* is the nearest to *T. baccata* in style and has some useful garden varieties. Other conifers that may be suitable are thuja and tsuga, because they have soft needles similar to those of taxus.

Thuja occidentalis 'Smaragd' (thuja, white cedar)

TYPE: Evergreen conifer
HEIGHT: 2m (6½ft)
SPREAD: 75cm (30in)
SEASONS OF INTEREST: Year-round foliage and form
CONDITIONS REQUIRED: Full sun and good drainage

This particular form of the white cedar has a lovely, rich green foliage. It is slow growing, but shows its conical shape from an early age. A good level of organic matter will be beneficial. It can be trimmed, but it is best left alone unless the odd spray of foliage is spoiling the overall shape.

IF YOU LIKE THIS PLANT, LOOK ALSO AT...
The other thujas. There are many garden forms of *Thuja occidentalis*, including 'Rheingold', which is a superb golden plant. *Thuja orientalis* also has many garden forms. If you are looking for conical plants, try junipers, particularly *Juniperus scopulorum* 'Skyrocket', and chamaecyparis, especially *C. lawsoniana* 'Lanei'. Tsugas may also be of interest.

Tsuga canadensis 'Jeddeloh'

TYPE: Evergreen conifer
HEIGHT: 30cm (12in)
SPREAD: 60cm (24in)
SEASONS OF INTEREST: Year-round foliage and form
CONDITIONS REQUIRED: Good drainage

This excellent dwarf conifer will do well in sun or light shade. The distinctive colour and form of this plant make a good feature for a rock garden or other smaller garden area. It looks very good set in gravel, but don't put it too close to a path because it will break if people brush by too closely.

IF YOU LIKE THIS PLANT, LOOK ALSO AT...
Other tsugas: *Tsuga canadensis* 'Pendula' is superb if you have the room, chamaecyparises and thujas also have soft foliage, although less needle-like. Cryptomerias may be worth seeking out. There are many dwarf junipers, picea and pinus that are similar to the tsuga here, the closest being *Picea abies* 'Nidiformis' (birds' nest spruce). *Picea abies* 'Little Gem' is similar but smaller growing.

Viburnum opulus 'Compactum' (guelder rose)

TYPE: Deciduous shrub
HEIGHT: 1.2m (4ft)
SPREAD: 1.2m (4ft)
SEASONS OF INTEREST: Spring flowers; autumn leaf colour and berries
CONDITIONS REQUIRED: Full sun and reasonable drainage

This plant will do well in any soil with a good level of organic matter, although it does not like to be too wet in winter. It can take shade, and indeed will be at its best in light shade rather than full sun in hotter summers. The habit of this plant alone makes it worth growing; the white flowers are an excellent feature but it is normally grown for its berries which complement the autumn coloration. There are other *Viburnum opulus* varieties, but they are a lot bigger.

IF YOU LIKE THIS PLANT, LOOK ALSO AT...
Other viburnums, particularly deciduous ones, such as *Viburnum carlesii*, *V.* × *juddii* and *V.* × *burkwoodii*. Sambucus may be of interest, although they tend to be larger. If the hummock form appeals, go for hebes, potentillas, *Genista lydia* and *Acer palmatum* or *A. japonicum*.

Choosing Plants

Choosing plants

These lists provide a broad guide to plants that give a certain type of display, such as winter flowers or autumn berries. They will also help you to select plants for a garden which presents a particular problem – dry or acidic soil, for example. They cannot be comprehensive lists, because new varieties are introduced every year; I have omitted some plants because I consider them inappropriate for this kind of book. Oak trees like alkaline soil, for example, but few of us have the space to do one justice. I have excluded tender plants completely. Still others may have been omitted because I am not aware of them yet!

The plants listed here do not fulfil the criteria established for the plants in the preceeding section of the book; they do not necessarily provide interest in more than one season.

Heuchera 'Plum Puddin'

Plants for acid soil

The plants listed here do not just like an acid soil; it is also important to have a large proportion of organic matter in the soil. Regular mulching is highly recommended as well.

Amelanchier canadensis
White flowers in spring, then orange-red leaf colour and dark fruits in the autumn.

Andromeda polifolia
A small, evergreen shrub which produces heather-like flowers.

Azalea
Now re-classified with the rhododendrons. There are two main types: large, deciduous shrubs (spectacular in spring and often with good autumn colour, too), and smaller, generally evergreen shrubs which are useful for the modern garden. This is a huge genus with many from which to choose. Watch out for tender varieties being sold outside in summer. Also, if they are on sale as houseplants, they are not hardy.

Calluna (heathers)
The UK's native heather, as seen on the Yorkshire moorlands. Quite a few varieties are available, all are summer-flowering.

Camellia
Medium to large evergreen shrubs. Deservedly popular for their flowers, although the latter can be lost if the buds are damaged by frost.

Cornus canadensis (dogwood)
An excellent ground-cover plant. Bears flowers and berries and has good autumn colour.

Cornus kousa var. *chinensis* (dogwood)
Spectacular when it flowers in June, this large shrub also has good autumn colour. Wonderful as a specimen plant in the middle of a lawn, it is good in the back of large borders. Underplant with spring/winter bulbs and you will have a display all year round.

Corylopsis
Medium-sized deciduous shrubs, related to hamamelis, but a bit more delicate in appearance.

Enkianthus campanulatus flowers in late spring

C. pauciflora is particularly recommended, the whole plant being covered with the cream-yellow flowers from early to mid-spring.

Cryptomeria
An evergreen conifer, but with soft foliage rather than needles. A wide variety is available. My recommendation is for *Cryptomeria japonica* 'Elegans Compacta' (Japanese cedar) (see page 43), but it can be hard to find.

Cypripedium reginae (lady's slipper orchid)
This hardy perennial needs a moist soil and shade to thrive and produce its dramatic white flowers.

Daboecia (Irish heather)
These have foliage that looks more leaf-like than that of the other heathers; otherwise they are similar. Flowers in the summer.

Daphne
Daphnes are almost unbeatable for late winter/early spring flowers, particularly *Daphne mezereum.* Otherwise they are not especially interesting, although there is an evergreen, variegated form called *Daphne odora* 'Aureo-marginata', and I rather like the way the bare branches look in winter.

Dierama pulcherrimum
This grass-like plant has beautiful deep red flowers in late summer/autumn. It needs moisture to thrive.

Enkianthus
This small genus contains shrubs that really are plants for all seasons. They flower in late spring with heather-like, bell-shaped blooms and later the dull green leaves see the year out with a bright red display of autumn colour. The most common variety is *Enkianthus campanulatus*, which is a large shrub.

Erica (heathers)
You can plant a whole garden with ericas and have flowers all through the year. They are also available as small shrubs, and even small trees, as well as the well-known heather-type plants. Many are worth growing for their foliage alone with the flowers as a bonus. *Erica carnea* and its varieties are lime tolerant. *Erica arborea* (tree heath) is an upright, shrub-like tree which was once used for making smokers' pipes. See page 46 for information and an illustration of *Erica × darleyensis*.

Eucryphia
This genus contains mostly small trees, although *Eucryphia × nymansensis* will grow to 14m (46ft) in time. The flowers are white, often fragrant, and some provide good autumn colour. May not be fully hardy in northern parts of UK.

Fothergilla
Deciduous shrubs with catkin-like flowers and superb autumn colour. *Fothergilla major* is a particularly recommended medium-sized shrub. *Fothergilla gardenii* is smaller (see page 47 for more information).

Gaultheria
Two main plants here, both good ground cover: *Gaultheria shallon* and *G. procumbens.* The latter is almost prostrate, while *Gaultheria shallon* is a small, rounded bush. Both are evergreen. There are a few other gaultheria, but none are as readily available as these two.

Gentiana (gentian)
Gentians can be difficult to grow but, as with all plants, if you give them the right conditions, they will thrive. They like sun or light shade and well-drained, moist soil with a high level of organic material.

Ginkgo biloba
This prehistoric tree is an unusual deciduous conifer. It turns a glorious yellow in autumn. The male form is more upright. One of my personal favourites.

Halesia carolina
A small, deciduous tree bearing flowers in late spring followed by green fruits. *Halesia monticola* is similar, but larger. Both prefer a sheltered spot.

Hamamelis (witch hazel)
The witch hazels are excellent, reliable flowering plants. All are large shrubs or small trees; they can be pruned smaller, but it spoils them. Recommended.

Hydrangea
Hydrangeas don't need an acid soil as a rule; a high level of organic matter is more important. However, you do need an acid soil to get blue flowers or true whites. Hydrangeas on an alkaline soil will be pink or at least flushed with pink. A huge range of small to large shrubs is available, all with superb flowers, but they do tend to look a mess in winter. *Hydrangea petiolaris* is an excellent climber, especially for shaded areas.

Iris
Irises can be grown in acid soils and need a high level of organic matter. Recommended.

Irises grow well in acid soil

Kalmia latifolia (calico bush)
The rich pink flowers on this evergreen shrub are an impressive sight. 'Ostbo Red' is a striking red-flowering variety. Both prefer to be positioned in full sun.

Larix (larches)
The larch is unusual for being a deciduous conifer. All are vigorous, fast-growing trees, hence their use in timber and paper production.

Leucothoe
Evergreen shrubs: *Leucothoe keiskei* is smallish reaching a height/spread of 60cm (24in), but *L. fontanesiana* is more dramatic with its arching branches. Both have white flowers.

Lewisia
These perennials are not for the gardener who likes to take things easy, because they need protection from the winter rain. However, they do have wonderful flowers.

Lilium (lilies)
Lilies can be grown in most soils, but they need a high level of organic matter. The best way to

Lilies can be grown in most soils

purchase them is as bulbs in late autumn/winter. Buy the largest bulbs you can. If you do buy plants in late spring/summer, make sure you purchase hardy types. Smaller varieties are suitable for pots.

Lupinus (lupin)
Generally hardy perennials, and these are the ones discussed here. New varieties coming out all the time. They have interesting foliage and reliable flowers, and can be grown in other soils so long as lots of organic matter is added.

Magnolia
Deciduous trees and shrubs with superb spring flowers. The most common types are *Magnolia* × *soulangeana*, *M. stellata* and *M. grandiflora*. The latter is semi-evergreen, retaining its leaves in most winters. There are many more; *Magnolia* × *loebneri* and its varieties are recommended. Buy one that is fragrant or you'll be missing out on one of their most delightful features.

Meconopsis (blue poppy)
The blue poppies need lots of organic matter. *Meconopsis betonicifolia* is one of the more reliable plants, but will still only live a few years. Superb flowers.

Narcissus cyclamineus
This species of daffodil is one of the earliest-flowering and needs a moist soil. Others can tolerate acid, but these are one of the best. Look at other species/varieties within the cyclaminens group.

Pachysandra terminalis
This is a plant for gardeners who like foliage. It is easy to grow, and can live quite happily in the deepest shade.

Pernettya
Grown for their berries, for which you will need both male and female plants. It is the female which bears the berries. Plant in a ratio of about four or five females to one male, fewer females if not planted in groups. They come in a range of berry colours, but most have white flowers. Evergreen, good ground cover.

Picea (spruce)
The spruces have not been as widely crossbred as other conifers, so there are not quite so many interesting or varied forms as there are with chamaecyparis, for example. However, you still get gold and blue plants, and everything from prostrate bushes to large trees. A particular favourite of mine is *Picea omorika*, a very narrow-growing tree. *Picea abies* (the UK's

native spruce and the common Christmas tree) has the most garden varieties.

Pieris
I cannot recommend this genus of evergreen shrubs highly enough. The profusion of bell-shaped blooms in early/mid-spring is superb. I also like the general habit of the plants and, being evergreen, they add structure to a winter garden. *Pieris* 'Forest Flame' is the most common variety and it deserves to be, but there are many more, and many are still being bred. They prefer light shade.

Pinus (pine)
There are some wonderful plants among the pines. One of my favourites is *Pinus strobus*, a tree whose needles form large whorls. *Pinus sylvestris* is the UK's Scots pine, which has been bred to produce some garden varieties: 'Doone Valley' is particularly good. Pines range from large trees to small shrubs.

Pleione formosana
This plant gets its common name, the garden orchid, from its exotic-looking flower. Bulbs are normally available from garden centres in the autumn.

Primula auricula
There are hundreds of different auriculas in a multitude of flower colours. Many are fragrant. Some other primulas also like acid conditions.

Rhododendron
These are evergreen shrubs, but they vary in size from very small, with a height and spread of under 30cm (12in), to huge reaching 10m (33ft) or more. Most garden varieties are about 2–4m (6½–13ft). I particularly like the compact plants, such as *Rhododendron × cilipense*, *R. impeditum*, and the Yakushimanum hybrids. All are excellent garden plants.

Rosa (rose)
Most roses will grow in a mildly acid soil as long as they have a lot of organic matter.

Sarcococca (Christmas box, sweet box)
Evergreen, winter-flowering shrubs. *Sarcococca hookeriana* var. *humilis* is the smallest, *S. ruscifolia* a bit larger and *S. hookeriana* the largest, with a height and spread of about 1.8m (6ft). They grow black berries after flowering, but these are not prominent.

Sciadopitys verticillata
With its quite unusual foliage, the slow-growing umbrella pine is an excellent talking point among garden visitors. From a distance it looks like a normal conifer.

Pieris 'Forest Flame'

Skimmia
Small, evergreen shrubs. Male and female plants are required if the females are to bear berries. People usually plant males because they have the more dramatic flowers. For best results, give them lots of organic matter and light shade.

Sorbus aucuparia (mountain ash, rowan)
This is a deservedly popular small tree for gardens. It provides good autumn colour and berries. See page 74 for more on *Sorbus aucuparia* 'Aspleniifolia'.

Mixed *Primula auricula*

Staphylea (bladdernut)
Spring-flowering large shrubs or small trees. All are deciduous.

Tricyrtis
The toad lilies are late summer/autumn-flowering hardy perennials. *Tricyrtis hirta* is particularly interesting. Some types have very interesting foliage.

Trillium
Trillium grandiflorum is one of my all-time favourite plants. All trilliums like an acid soil; most have red or white flowers; some are fragrant. All need at least light shade.

Tropaeolum speciosum
A climber that is not fully hardy in northern parts of the UK. It should manage in a sheltered spot and looks good grown through other plants.

Vinca
Vinca major and *V. minor* will grow in acid soils as long as they have lots of organic matter. They prefer light shade. Spreading, prostrate (or trailing), they look good over walls and as ground cover under roses. Evergreen.

Trillium grandiflorum in flower

Plants for alkaline soil

The plants listed here are not just alkaline-lovers; they are suitable for most garden soils. Regular mulching is highly recommended.

Acer species & varieties
Except for the Japanese maples (*Acer palmatum* and *A. japonicum*), all of the readily available acers are recommended. They are excellent small trees, and many have interesting bark (see page 28). *Acer campestre*, *A. cappadocicum* and *A. griseum* are particularly recommended. *Acer negundo* and its varieties can be large shrubs. *Acer negundo* 'Flamingo' is featured on page 27.

Ailanthus altissima
The tree of heaven is a large, fast-growing tree. It can be cut down hard each winter to make a shrub, thus emphasizing the attractive foliage. Goes a vivid yellow in autumn.

Alnus species
Some alders, such as *Alnus glutinosa* 'Imperialis', make excellent small trees, but most are large. They bear woody cones after a good catkin display in early spring. All are easy to grow and like damp situations.

Amelanchier lamarckii
An outstanding shrub or small tree which is featured on page 30.

Arbutus unedo
The fruits of the strawberry tree look like strawberries when you get close to them. It flowers in late autumn and bears fruit the following year. It is slow-growing and a good choice for any garden.

Arundinaria
Like most bamboos, arundinaria will live on alkaline soils. It is important to add large quantities of organic matter to the soil.

Berberis species
You can take your pick from this large genus. They come as deciduous or evergreen, with coloured foliage, as large or small shrubs, with different flower colours (although most are yellow) and with berries. The thorns put some people off, but they are recommended. *Berberis × carminea* 'Buccaneer' and *B. darwinii* are discussed on pages 31 and 32 respectively.

Betula species
All birch trees are suitable and vary from small to large trees; some have outstanding bark. Generally elegant in appearance and highly recommended.

Buddleia species
A range of large, deciduous shrubs with superb flowers.

Callicarpa bodinieri var. 'Profusion'
This shrub will reach a height of 2m (6½ft), but retains a narrow form. It has pink flowers in late summer, followed by autumn berries and colour.

Carpinus betulus (common hornbeam)
A smaller-growing tree, it will eventually grow to around 8m (30ft) tall and 6m (20ft) wide. It is often used in hedges. Different varieties give different colours and shapes. The foliage of 'Purpurea' displays lovely purple hues in spring and again in autumn. Recommended.

Catalpa bignonioides (Indian bean tree)
If you like big oval leaves, this is for you! It flowers quite dramatically in spring (or summer), with white, bell-shaped flowers marked with yellow and purple, then bears its runner bean-like fruit in the autumn. A good talking point for the garden, if you have room, as it can grow to a height and spread of 10m (33ft).

Callicarpa bodinieri var. 'Profusion' in berry

Choisya ternata
A large, evergreen shrub which forms a distinctive, rounded mound. The foliage is aromatic when rubbed or crushed. There is also a good, golden form, *Choisya ternata* 'Sundance' (see page 34).

Cistus species
A range of evergreen shrubs of various sizes. They need a well-drained soil. Superb flowers.

Corylus species
There are two main types of hazel: *Corylus*

colurna, the Turkish hazel, and the one native to the UK, *C. avellana*. Both are recommended as large shrubs or small trees. *Corylus avellana* 'Contorta' is featured on page 39.

Cotoneaster species
This large genus offers a great choice. There are deciduous and evergreen examples, some with coloured foliage, large and small shrubs, different flower colours (though most are white) and berries. Some varieties, such as *Cotoneaster horizontalis* (featured on page 40), are very common but deservedly so. Recommended.

Crataegus species
Crataegus is the genus of *Crataegus monogyna*, the UK's native hawthorn. All are large shrubs or small trees which flower in late spring. *Crataegus laevigata (oxyacantha)* 'Crimson Cloud' is particularly recommended for its mass of flowers – it was well named!

Crataegus laevigata 'Crimson Cloud' in flower

Daphne species
These small shrubs need good drainage to survive. *Daphne mezereum* has superb, deep red winter flowers. *Daphne × burkwoodii* bears pink flowers in late spring.

Davidia involucrata (handkerchief tree)
An aptly named plant, but it will take a few years to bear the large, white bracts (a specialized leaf) that give this small to medium-sized tree its common name. Recommended.

Deutzia species
A genus of deciduous shrubs that flower early in the summer. Popular because they are reliable and easy to grow.

Elaeagnus species
Large, evergreen shrubs grown for their foliage. See *Elaeagnus pungens* 'Maculata' on page 45.

Escallonia species
This group of evergreen shrubs may lose their leaves in a hard winter. There is a wide range of sizes available, although most reach a height and spread of 1.5–2m (5–6½ft). Most varieties have pink flowers, but reds and whites are also grown.

Euonymus species
This genus is deservedly well known for its evergreen, ground-cover varieties, such as *Euonymus fortunei* 'Emerald Gaiety' and 'Emerald and Gold', but there is a range of different foliage plants. There are also a few deciduous varieties which can make good garden oddities; a couple have excellent autumn colour (see the list of plants for autumn colour on page 95).

Euonymus fortunei 'Emerald Gold'

Fagus species (beech)
There are many varieties of beech tree; some can be treated as large shrubs, but most turn into handsome trees.

Forsythia species
Forsythia must be one of the most popular spring-flowering shrubs. It is a shame that it doesn't flower for longer or have other features, but it is easy to grow and reliable.

Fraxinus excelsior (common ash)
The ash tree is a splendid, large, fast-growing, tree, but there are varieties which are smaller. There are also some ornamental types, such as *Fraxinus excelsior* 'Aurea Pendula', a golden form.

Fuchsia species
Be aware that there are hardy and tender fuchsias. The latter can be excellent as bedding plants and in hanging baskets. Hardy plants of note are *Fuchsia* 'Tom Thumb' with pink flowers growing up to 60cm (24in), *F.* 'Mrs

Popple', the most hardy, reaching up to 1.8m (6ft) with the traditional purple/blue fuchsia flower, and *F.* 'Madame Cornelissen', up to 90cm (36in) high and 1.2m (4ft) wide with red and white flowers. *Fuchsia magellanica* is featured on page 48. Fuchsias are highly recommended for their length of flowering. All are deciduous, possibly even dying back to the ground each winter. Prune out any dead wood in the spring, once the leaves have started growing.

Gleditsia triacanthos
This tree will eventually grow to over 8m (26ft) tall, but much more worthy of garden interest are some of its many varieties. Of particular note are 'Sunburst' (a smaller-growing, golden form), 'Elegantissima' (a smaller, more elegant form) and 'Rubylace' (smaller growing, with ruby-coloured new growth).

Gypsophila species
Gypsophila repens or *G. paniculata* are the best gypsophilas, being hardy perennials, but there are also annuals and some of the other perennials are worth considering. They all need good drainage.

Hedera species
All ivies are tolerant of a wide range of conditions. There are a few varieties that are not climbers. Only *Hedera helix* (the UK's native ivy) and its varieties are self-clinging; the rest will need some form of support, such as a trellis. *Hedera helix* 'Glacier' is featured on page 53.

Hibiscus species
These deciduous shrubs often come into leaf very late in the spring and flower late in the summer. They usually have blue flowers, but others are available.

Kerria japonica
An elegant, almost bamboo-like shrub up to 2m (6½ft) tall. Unfortunately, it is more usually found in the smaller-growing, double-flowered variety 'Pleniflora'. There is also a variegated form.

Kolkwitzia amabilis 'Pink Cloud'
Featured on page 57. Recommended.

Laburnum × watereri 'Vossii'
This form of laburnum has bigger flowers than the normal type and has very few of the poisonous seed pods in the autumn. It also tends to be quite erect in habit.

Liriodendron tulipifera
This large tree covered with tulip-like flowers in the summer is an amazing sight. Unfortunately, it only really flowers well as a mature specimen. However, the interesting foliage and excellent autumn colour help make the wait worthwhile. A great plant if you have the room.

Malus species
The crab apples are large shrubs or small trees. The spring flower display is excellent and most get at least some autumn colour – and apples – of course. Recommended.

Olearia species
These evergreen shrubs all have fragrant, white flowers in summer. Recommended.

Liriodendron tulipifera gives good autumn colour

Pyrus salicifolia 'Pendula' cascading to the ground

Paeonia delavayi
This type of tree peony forms a rounded mound of attractive foliage up to 2m (6½ft) high and 1.2m (4ft) across. The dramatic spring flowering is usually followed by dark fruits in autumn.

Paulownia tomentosa
This small to medium tree is mostly grown for its distinctive foliage, although mature trees will flower in May. It can be pruned hard in winter to keep it as a shrub.

Philadelphus species
This genus of deciduous shrubs is grown for their fragrant, white flowers in late spring/early summer. The mock oranges come in a range of sizes from 1.2–3m (4–10ft).

Potentilla species
This genus comprises a huge range of shrubs and herbaceous perennials; all will live on alkaline soils. The shrubs are worthy of note for the length and reliability of their flowering. *Potentilla fruticosa* 'Elizabeth' is covered in more detail on page 68.

Prunus species
This genus covers the flowering cherries, of which there are many very good varieties; most are small to medium trees. It also includes *Prunus laurocerasus* (laurel) and its varieties, which make good foliage shrubs.

Pyracantha species
This genus is most well known for the berries produced prolifically each autumn. However, the spring flowering (usually white) is also of note. See *Pyracantha* 'Orange Charmer' on page 70.

Spiraea

Pyrus species
There are many good ornamental pear trees. Of particular note are *Pyrus calleryana* 'Chanticleer' (see page 71) and *P. salicifolia* 'Pendula'. The latter is a superb silver-leafed, weeping tree which, if left unpruned, will become a dense bush ideal for nesting birds.

Ribes
The flowering currants are excellent spring-flowering plants. See page 72 for more on *Ribes odoratum* and page 99 for a berry-bearing plants .

Robinia pseudoacacia
This light, open tree will get very large. More suitable for garden use is the excellent variety 'Frisia'. This has golden foliage and is smaller growing. It has fragrant, white flowers in June.

Santolina species
A genus of small shrubs. Of particular note are *Santolina virens* with glossy green, heather-like foliage, yellow flowers, and growing up to 45cm (18in) tall and *S. chamaecyparissus* with grey/silver foliage, yellow flowers, growing up to 45cm (18in) tall.

Sorbus aria 'Lutescens'
A superb small tree with silvery foliage.

Spartium junceum (Spanish broom)
The Spanish broom is quite spectacular when in flower in late June/July and for the rest of the year has glossy green, brush-like foliage. Plant with cytisus and genista varieties for a longer flowering season.

Syringa meyeri 'Palibin' in full flower

Spiraea species
Spiraeas are extremely tough, deciduous shrubs. Their ability to cope with damage does not mean that they are ugly plants, however; they have some of the best summer flowering of any shrubs. Try *Spiraea* × *arguta* (white spring flowers, up to 2m (6½ft) tall), *S.* × *bumalda* 'Shirobane' (white and pink/red flowers July onwards, up to 1.2m (4ft) tall) and *S. nipponica* 'Snowmound' (white flowers in June, dense mound up to 90cm (36in) tall). *Spiraea* x *bumalda* 'Gold Mound' is featured on page 76.

Symphoricarpos species
This genus is mostly grown for its white 'snowberries' and comprises a range of deciduous shrubs around 1.5m (5ft) tall.

Syringa species
Lilacs are probably the most famous plants for

alkaline soils. Most of the species, and hybrids, are huge shrubs, but *Syringa meyeri* 'Palibin' will reach only 1.2m (4ft) and *S. microphylla* 'Superba' will reach 1.5m (5ft).

Tamarix species
Tamarisks are large, feathery-looking shrubs up to 3.5m (11½ft). They all bear pink flowers in late summer. Recommended if you have the room.

Teucrium fruticans
A grey-leafed shrub up to 1.2m (4ft) tall with blue flowers in midsummer. There is also a smaller form, Teucrium *fruticans* 'Compactum' which will reach 60–75cm (24–30in). Recommended.

Viburnum species
A large genus of evergreen and deciduous shrubs. Various flowering seasons, colours (mostly white) and sizes. Various species appear in other lists in this book and *Viburnum opulus* 'Compactum' is featured on page 80.

Vinca species
The two main types, *Vinca major* and *V. minor*, differ mostly in their size. For both, a variegated form is available. They make good ground- and object-covering plants.

Weigela species
This genus contains early-summer-flowering, deciduous shrubs. They are popular because they are easy to grow, hardy and reliable.

Yucca species
Yuccas are good for adding something different form-wise to your garden. They are mainly grown for their tropical-looking foliage, but they do flower if given a reasonably warm spring/summer. They make excellent container-grown plants.

Yucca gloriosa 'Tricolor'

Plants for autumn colour

Here is a list of plants whose foliage changes colour in the autumn and then usually drops off. However, not all of them lose their leaves. Many grasses, conifers and ivies change colour before the onset of winter; these have not been listed, except for *Cryptomeria*. There are also many plants that bring forth berries or flowers in the autumn.

Acer ginnala
Fiery red autumn colour, yellow flowers in May. A lovely small tree.

Ailanthus altissima
The tree of heaven is a large fast-growing tree. It can be pruned (very) hard to keep it as a shrub.

Amelanchier lamarckii
An outstanding shrub/small tree. See page 30.

Azalea (deciduous varieties)
The deciduous azaleas are very like the evergreen rhododendrons and azaleas to which they are closely related, but they are much more open in habit. They are grown for their spectacular spring flowering, but their autumn coloration can be equally stunning. All need an acid soil.

The autumn leaves of *Cercidiphyllum japonicum* provide a stunning display

Acer palmatum var. *heptalobum* 'Osakazuki'
A superstar, even amongst the outstanding shrub-type maples, with its autumn colour of brilliant orange/red. See *Acer palmatum* on page 28.

Acer saccharinum (and varieties)
These are the trees that create the beautiful New England 'falls'. Most are small to medium sized trees. This one is a slender tree, pretty in spring/summer. Most acers can be relied on to give good autumn colour.

Berberis × *carminea* 'Buccaneer'
See page 31.

Berberis wilsoniae
Most deciduous berberis give good autumn colour. *Berberis wilsoniae* is a small shrub which flowers in July, but is really grown for its berries. An excellent plant for ground cover.

Betula species and varieties
Most birch trees give good autumn colour and are elegant throughout spring and summer, only casting light shade. They also have attractive bark.

Callicarpa bodinieri var. 'Profusion'
This shrub will reach 2m (6½ft) in height, but remains narrower. The autumn colour is complemented by the berries. It also has pink flowers in late summer.

Ceratostigma willmottianum
A small shrub whose dying red foliage is usually late and follows the blue flowers which are held into autumn. There are other ceratostigma, including perennial forms, all of which are worthy of attention.

Cercidiphyllum japonicum
The katsura tree must have lime-free soil, which is a shame, because it would otherwise be a far more popular large shrub/small tree. The young foliage is a spectacle in spring and the autumn colour is a treat.

Cornus canadensis
Featured on page 36.

Cornus mas and *C. kousa chinensis* (dogwoods)
These two dogwoods are both excellent large shrubs or small trees. They require a soil rich in organic matter.

Cotinus coggygria and varieties (smoke bush)
The smoke bush is a superb large shrub, available in purple-leafed form. All are covered in 'smoke' (flowers) in the summer although older plants give a better display. *Cotinus coggygria* Purpureus probably gives the best autumn colour, turning fiery orange-red before dropping.

Cotoneaster species
Cotoneasters are evergreen but some do have coloured autumn foliage, or even lose their leaves if the weather is cold enough. *Cotoneaster bullatus*, *C. divaricatus*, *C. rotundifolius* and *C. simonsii* are best for autumn colour. Most cotoneasters produce berries in the autumn.

Cotinus coggygria Purpureus bears unusual flowers

Cryptomeria japonica and varieties
This conifer does not actually lose its foliage. Cryptomeria japonica 'Elegans' is featured on page 43.

Enkianthus campanulatus
Superb autumn colour with flowers in May. Needs acid soil.

Euonymus latifolius
Brilliant red autumn colour on an otherwise not very interesting large shrub which grows up to 3m (10ft) tall. *Euonymus alatus* is similar but smaller. *Euonymus europaeus* 'Red Cascade' is inbetween the two in size, around 1.5m (5ft) high and wide, and gives more of a show with its fruits.

Fagus sylvatica 'Dawyck'
A narrow-growing tree, which, like most beech trees, can retain its leaves after they have turned in the autumn. This variety is smaller than most, growing to only 7m (23ft) and the foliage turns a copper colour.

Fothergilla species
A genus of small to large shrubs, all requiring acid soil. Generally excellent autumn colour; most have bottlebrush-type flowers in spring.

Ginkgo biloba
This prehistoric tree has distinctive leaves which fade to yellow in the autumn and are held on the tree longer than on most plants.

The yellow autumn leaves of *Ginkgo biloba*

Hamamelis mollis (witch hazel)
The witch hazel needs a soil rich in organic matter. It grows into a large shrub or small tree and flowers in the winter. Varieties are available.

Liquidambar styraciflua
As this sweet gum's Latin name suggests, its leaves do indeed turn the colour of liquid amber.

Liriodendron tulipifera (tulip tree)
The tulip tree is named after the shape of its foliage which colours brilliantly in the autumn. A large, slow-growing tree.

Lythrum salicaria
Featured on page 59.

Nandina domestica
An evergreen shrub which colours red for the autumn/winter. See *Nandina domestica* 'Firepower' on page 61.

Parrotia persica
This large, winter-flowering shrub or small tree turns multi-coloured in the autumn. For best results, it needs a soil high in organic matter, preferably acid.

Parthenocissus species and varieties
These climbers do bear some flowers and berries, but are grown primarily for their foliage and superb autumn colour. *Parthenocissus tricuspidata* and its varieties are the best.

Prunus species and varieties
Many of the flowering cherries will give good colour before dropping their leaves. Most are small trees suitable for all kinds of gardens. See *Prunus* 'Shirofugen' on page 69.

Pyrus calleryana 'Chanticleer'
Featured on page 71.

Ribes alpinum
This small flowering currant turns orange/red in the autumn. It produces yellow flowers in April/May.

Ribes odoratum
Featured on page 72.

Robinia pseudoacacia
This small tree is deservedly popular with modern gardeners. It flowers in early summer. The pinnate foliage is a pale green all summer and turns yellow in the autumn.

Sorbus species
Nearly all the sorbus species are excellent small trees; some have interesting bark, most are grown for their flowers and/or berries. All colour well in the autumn, as do some of the varieties. See *Sorbus aucuparia* 'Aspleniifolia' on page 74.

Spiraea species and varieties
Most spiraea colour in the autumn. Of note are *Spiraea japonica* 'Alpina' and *S. prunifolia* 'Plena'.

Sorbus aucuparia in autumn colour

Stephanandra incisa 'Crispa'
This low-growing plant has attractive leaves which remain interesting as they turn brown. It has white flowers in June.

Taxodium disticum (swamp cypress)
This deciduous conifer is recommended if you have the space, reaching 30m (100ft).

Vaccinium species
This genus of shrubs needs an acid soil. Most turn orange/red in the autumn and flower in spring.

Viburnum carlesii and *V. lantana*
These two plants are fairly large, open shrubs. *Viburnum carlesii* will turn red or yellow; *V. lantana* will go crimson. Both also bear flowers and berries.

Viburnum plicatum 'Lanarth'
With its layers of horizontal branches, this outstanding plant has a useful 'architectural' quality. The darkening of the leaves before they drop is a bonus.

Vitis
All the plants in this genus of climbers give superb autumn colour. If you want grapes as well, *Vitis vinifera* 'Brant' is one of the best for growing in the UK.

Viburnum plicatum 'Lanarth' lends form as well as colour to a garden

Plants for berries

Berries are fruits. Some are edible, even on ornamental plants, such as chaenomeles (quince). The majority are decorative, however, giving another season of interest. They also provide a good source of food for the local birds and so help to make the garden more interesting as well as environmentally friendly. All of the plants listed here are suitable for the gardener with limited time, subject to the usual proviso about giving the plant the right conditions.

Amelanchier lamarckii
Featured on page 30.

Arbutus unedo (strawberry tree)
The fruits of this tree look like strawberries from a distance. It flowers in late autumn for fruit the following year. It is an excellent slow-growing, large shrub or small tree.

Arctostaphylos uva-ursi
A dwarf, trailing plant that requires acid soil. Red fruits.

The eye-catching fruit of *Arbutus unedo*

Berberis
A genus of numerous varieties of evergreen and deciduous shrubs of various sizes. Most like sun and dry conditions; all berry well. *Berberis darwinii* and *B.* × *carminea* 'Buccaneer' are featured on pages 31 and 32.

Chaenomeles (Cydonia) (quince)
Bears edible fruits which are usually made into quince jelly. Medium to large shrubs with early spring flowers that are usually red, but can sometimes be pink or white. Recommended. See *Chaenomeles* x *superba* 'Rowallane' on page 33.

Cotoneaster
All varieties berry, but the following are recommended: *Cotoneaster* × watereri 'Cornubia', with a height and spread of 3m (10ft), and a prolific producer of bright red berries); *C. dammeri (humifusus)*, a prostrate plant with bright red berries; *C. horizontalis,* with a fish bone structure to the branches, and scarlet berries; *C.* × *rothchildianus* up to 3m (10ft) high and across, with yellow berries.

Crataegus (hawthorn)
Crataegus monogyna, the United Kingdom's native hawthorn, makes an excellent hedge or small tree. Recommended also are *Crataegus laevigata (oxycantha)* 'Rosea Flore Pleno' and *C. laevigata (oxycantha)* 'Crimson Cloud' for their superb flowering and berries.

Daphne mezereum
A shrub grown for its winter/early spring flowers; the scarlet berries are a bonus. Needs moist soil and light shade.

Gaultheria procumbens
A prostrate evergreen requiring an acid soil.

Halesia
Halesia carolina and *H. monticola* are spring-flowering trees requiring an acid soil. The flowers are followed by green fruits.

Ilex (hollies)
Please note that with all hollies you need male and female plants present if the female is to bear berries. They make excellent hedges, large shrubs or small trees. There are many types available, including some with variegated or blue foliage.

Mahonia
Mostly grown for their brilliant yellowflowers in winter; the blue/black berries that form afterwards are also interesting.

Malus (crab apples)
These are small trees that produce fruit you can make into wine or jelly. 'John Downie' is especially good for this. 'Golden Hornet' is bright yellow. 'Red Sentinel' a cardinal red. 'Royalty' is a deep red, *M. sargentii* is bright red, and *M. yunnanesis* 'Veitch's Scarlet' is unsurprisingly scarlet!

Osmanthus decorus
An evergreen, medium-sized shrub bearing fragrant, white flowers in mid-spring followed by dark purple berries.

Pernettya
These plants must have an acid soil. You need

Malus 'Veitch's Scarlet' (crab apple)

male and female plants to get the extremely dramatic berries. There are lots of colours available and they do well in pots, as long as they don't dry out.

Pyracantha
Pyracanthas are easy to grow and can be trained as climbers or wall shrubs. All varieties produce berries, but the following are recommended: *Pyracantha* 'Mohave' (orange/red), *P. rogersiana, P. gibbsii* 'Flava' (yellow), and *P.* 'Teton' (yellow/orange). *Pyracantha* 'Orange Charmer' is featured on page 70.

Ribes
Flowering currants are excellent plants for the busy gardener, tolerating most conditions and giving superb spring flowers. *Ribes sanguineum* 'Pulborough Scarlet' is a particularly recommended large shrub. *Ribes odoratum* is featured on page 72.

Rosa species
Try *Rosa forrestiana*, *R. illiensis*, *R. macrophyla*, *R. moyesii*, *R. nitida*, *R. pomifera*, *R. rugosa*, *R. rugosa* 'Alba', *R. sweginzowi*, *R. woodsii* var. *fendleri* and their varieties. Particularly recommended as all-rounders are *Rosa moyesii* 'Geranium' (see page 73) and *Rosa* 'Fru Dagmar Hastrup'.

Sarcococca
Bears winter flowers followed by black berries which are not very obvious.

Skimmia
These plants need acid soil. The male plants are extremely showy during flowering and are the most commonly sold for that reason. You need to have plants of both sexes present to get the red berries on the female plants.

Sorbus
All small trees. All are excellent garden plants that fruit well. *Sorbus aria* 'Lutescens' has a lovely shape, foliage with silver undersides and berries that are cherry red. *Sorbus cashmiriana* is another beautiful tree bearing white berries that are flushed with pink. *Sorbus vilmorinii* has deep pink berries which fade to almost white. *Sorbus aucuparia* (rowan or mountain ash) has red berries. *Sorbus aucuparia* 'Aspleniifolia' is featured on page 74.

Staphylea colchica
A large, deciduous shrub with greenish-white fruits after flowering in late spring. Needs soil, preferably acid, with lots of organic matter.

Symplocarpus (snowberry)
Snowberries produce white, squishy fruits in mid to late summer after insignificant flowering.

Viburnum
An excellent genus of shrubs, both evergreen and deciduous, and of varying sizes. Most berry, but not all. Of note are: *V. davidii*, *V. opulus* and varieties, and *V. lantana*. *V. rhytidophyllum* is also of interest. Although its berries are not so prominent, it is an interesting large shrub.

Viburnum davidii bears dark berries

Plants for boggy areas

The majority of plants in this list require soil that does not dry out in the summer. The easiest way of ensuring this is to incorporate a great deal of organic matter before planting and mulch regularly afterwards. For actual bog plants, you can dig a shallow (one spit depth) hole over the area you wish to make into the bog garden, and then line the bottom and sides of the hole with plastic or an old pond liner to approximately 2.5–5cm (1–2in) below the surface. It doesn't matter if there are small holes or overlaps in the plastic; you do not want to create a pond. For best results, the soil used to back-fill the hole should be about 50 per cent organic matter. It is not necessary to use this method for large plants, shrubs for example, because they can get the depth of root to resist drought. Most plants that need an acid soil also need moisture and organic matter.

Acer negundo and varieties
A fast-growing, but small, tree (up to 9m (29½ft). *Acer negundo* 'Flamingo' can be found on page 27.

Acer palmatum and varieties
The Japanese maples are delightful, large shrubs. They need shade to avoid leaf scorch. *Acer palmatum* 'Dissectum' is featured on page 28.

Alchemilla mollis
This form of lady's mantle has interesting green flowers in summer. It is a perennial, reaching a height of 60cm (24in) and spreads readily by seed.

Amelanchier lamarckii
Featured on page 30.

Aruncus dioicus (goatsbeard)
The common name of this plant gives you a good idea of what the white flowers look like. It is a perennial with a height of 2m (6½ft) and a spread of 1.2m (4ft).

Aster species and varieties
There are hundreds of different Michaelmas daisies, but not all are hardy. The species *Aster nova-belgii* and its varieties are particularly recommended, although they sometimes need spraying with a fungicide to prevent mildew.

Astilbe × *arendsii* 'Fanal'

Astilbe species and varieties
Astilbes need light shade for best results. I feel they are worth growing for their ferny foliage alone, the unusual flowers in summer being a superb bonus. They vary from 15cm–1m (6in–3¼ft) in height and all are clump-forming perennials.

Aucuba japonica and varieties
These evergreen shrubs are tolerant of virtually all garden conditions. The variegated forms make a good backdrop for other plants and all of them make excellent hedges.

Betula pendula and varieties (birches)
The birch is one of the most elegant trees available for the gardener. It is also useful in that it does not cast heavy shade. Some varieties are large shrubs.

Caltha palustris and varieties
The marsh marigold likes so much moisture that it can be grown in a pond, but a moist soil is better. A perennial, there are quite a few varieties, with yellow or white flowers.

Cercidiphyllum japonicum (katsura tree)
Worth growing for its autumn colour alone, although the young foliage is also interesting. Best on an acid soil.

Cornus species and varieties (dogwoods)
The archetypal damp-soil shrubs. The most well known, *Cornus alba* and *C. stolonifera* and their varieties, are grown for the colour of their winter bark, but there is a wide range of shrubs and trees with excellent flowering. Some need an acid soil. *Cornus canadensis* is featured on page 36.

Elaeagnus × *ebbingei*
This large, blue-leafed, evergreen shrub is fast growing. Its white, summer flowers are not prominent, but they are fragrant. It makes an excellent hedge.

Fatsia japonica
This shrub's large, evergreen leaves make a dramatic feature all year round. It needs shade for best results and can be damaged by cold winds in winter. It will reach up to 3m (10ft) in both height and spread.

Fatsia japonica

Dicksonia antarctica

Ferns
There are a large number of hardy ferns available to the gardener, especially as their popularity has increased in the late 1990s. Any good garden centre should have a selection, but to find certain kinds you will have to visit a specialist. Good genus to look for are dryopteris, polystichum, polypodium and adiantum. Ferns can vary in size from tiny to tree-like. If they interest you, it is well worth visiting a botanic garden to get a glimpse of a mature *Dicksonia antarctica.*

Filipendula species and varieties
Similar to astilbes, this genus of perennials is however less common and will grow more successfully in full sun. They tend to be bigger than astilbes; although there are varieties that are 60cm (24in) tall, the tallest are up to 1.8m (6ft).

Fothergilla species and varieties
This small genus of shrubs all produce bottlebrush-like flowers in late spring, but the autumn coloration of their leaves is the real show. They need full sun or light shade and an acid soil. *Fothergilla major* reaches a height of up to 2m (6½ft). *Fothergilla gardenii* is smaller (see page 47).

Fritillaria meleagris and varieties
The snake's-head fritillary is an unusual bulb because it tolerates wet soils. It is excellent in lawns and works well planted underneath trees and taller shrubs.

Gunnera manicata
A true pond or bog plant, this extremely dramatic perennial is only for the larger garden. You will see it in most parks and gardens with lakes. The huge leaves grow up to 3m (10ft) tall and the cones produced underneath can be up to 2m (6½ft) long. Superb if you have the room.

Hamamelis species and varieties (witch hazels)
Witch hazels all need an acid soil. This genus of large, deciduous shrubs, up to 3–4m (10–13ft) tall, is well worth growing for their fragrant, winter/early spring flowers.

Helleborus species and varieties (hellebores)
This genus of perennials includes the Christmas rose (*Helleborus niger*), a good example of these

plants. Although perennial, it keeps its leaves over the winter and the new leaves replace them in the spring. Most hellebores are winter/early spring flowering. *Helleborus orientalis* and its varieties are also recommended.

Hemerocallis species and varieties
Daylilies have been bred a lot, so there are numerous varieties available. Most are shades of yellow, but white, orange and red are also grown. All are 30–90cm (12–36in) tall and clump forming. Recommended if you like large flowers.

Hosta species and varieties
Hostas are grown for their superb foliage, but they do flower in summer/autumn, mostly lavender blue. All of the thousands of varieties do best in light shade, but some with all-green leaves will do fine in full sun. They also do well as container-grown subjects.

Houttuynia cordata and varieties
If this plant is happy it can become a problem because it spreads so rapidly. Don't let this dissuade you from planting it, because it is easily controlled by pulling up the excess. It also makes a good container plant, because it tolerates drying out. It can be grown in ponds or bog gardens. The most well-known variety is 'Chameleon', which spreads more slowly and has a striking red/white variegated leaf.

Hydrangea macrophylla varieties
Deciduous shrubs, famous for their big pink, white or blue flowerheads. There are two main types: 'lace caps' and 'mop heads'. The former are quite delicate; the latter tend to give more colour. Both are represented by a huge number of varieties. A good example of a lace cap is *Hydrangea macrophylla* 'Blue Wave'; the mop heads include *H. serrata* 'Preziosa'. The colour of the flowers will vary depending on the pH of your soil: pink on alkaline and blue on acid.

Hydrangea species and varieties
Hydrangea shrubs grow very large, except *Hydrangea villosa* and *H. quercifolia* which reach 2m (6½ft) and 1.5m (5ft) respectively. Both have white flowers (although *H. villosa* can have other coloration), and give good

Gunnera manicata needs a large area

Hemerocallis 'Golden Chimes'

autumn colour. Also of note is *Hydrangea petiolaris*, a deciduous climber. It is one of the best plants for a shaded wall (see page 55).

Iris species and varieties
Irises are tolerant of a wide range of conditions in the garden. There are thousands of varieties, varying in height from a few centimetres to 1m (3¼ft) high, and there are all kinds of colours. You should double-check with the label that your particular purchase will be suitable for the site you have chosen; reticulata types, for example, will not like a soggy soil in winter.

Liquidambar styraciflua
The sweet gum is a beautiful, maple-like tree which grows up to 20m (66ft) high. It has superb autumn colour and interesting bark. There are smaller varieties available.

Liquidambar styraciflua (sweet gum)

Liriodendron tulipifera
A tulip tree in summer, covered with white, tulip-like flowers, is a spectac lar sight. It reaches up to 30m (100ft) in height. The foliage is quite unusual too and goes a pleasant yellow before it drops in the winter.

Lysimachia punctata
This perennial looks superb in early to midsummer, with yellow flowers covering the stems. It reaches up to 90cm (36in) in height and is clump forming. Recommended for a mixed border.

Lysimachia punctata in full flower

Lythrum salicaria
Featured on page 59.

Monarda didyma and varieties
Bergamot is worth growing even if you do not intend to make use of its herbal properties. A clump-forming perennial, it will reach a maximum of 1m (3¼ft) in height with the flowers above the foliage. *M.* 'Cambridge Scarlet' has superb red flowers.

Pachysandra terminalis
This interesting evergreen plant reaches up to 30cm (12in) height. It will grow in even the darkest shade and is often used under trees or buildings in parks and gardens. It has no flowers, but there is a variegated form.

Physocarpus opulifolius and varieties
This deciduous shrub needs full sun. It will reach up to 3m (10ft) high and 5m (16½ft) across. *Physocarpus opulifolius* 'Luteus' is smaller – (height: 2m (6½ft); spread: 1.5m (5ft) – and has golden foliage. In summer both have white flowers that may develop a pinkish tinge during some years. Both types develop an interesting peeling bark.

Pieris species and varieties
These evergreen shrubs are grown for the fabulous spring colours of the new foliage and flowers. Variegated forms help give year-round interest. They all need an acid soil. The majority are around 3m (10ft) in height, but there are dwarf forms available.

Polygonum species and varieties (knotweeds)
An extremely varied genus, which includes the Russian vine (a large, fast-growing climber), annuals and perennials. The latter are of particular interest here. *Polygonum affine* and its varieties are popular, but *P. amplexicaule*, *P. bistorta* 'Superbum', *P. campanulatum* and *P. vaccinifolium* are also worthy of attention.

Primula species and varieties
Primulas are probably most well known as bedding plants for late winter/spring flowering. However, most of the plants sold for this use are in fact hardy perennials which can be left in the garden year after year. However, they do not tend to look very good in summer. I get around this by planting summer-flowering bulbs and other plants with them. One of the best plants to put with these are the summer-flowering primulas, such as *Primula japonica* 'Millers Crimson' or *P. pulverulenta*. These are both 'candelabra' primulas which refers to the circles of flowers up the stems. There are hundreds of different primulas available, including auriculas which are a bit more specialized. They tend to need more care than most primulas, but reward this with some very unusual and spectacular flowers.

A candelabra primula

Prunus laurocerasus and varieties
This plant is normally seen as one of two varieties: 'Otto Luyken' or 'Zabeliana'. Both are evergreen shrubs up to 1.2m (4ft) high and 1.8m (6ft) wide. They bear white flowers in April/May, but they are not prominent. They make excellent ground cover, and form a good low hedge.

Pyrus calleryana 'Chanticleer'
Featured on page 71.

Rodgersia species and varieties
These perennials have interesting foliage, but they also all flower in summer. Most are white or cream, but *Rodgersia pinnata* 'Superba' has excellent pink flowers. They are all about 1–1.2m (3¼–4ft) high and clump forming.

Salix species and varieties
Willows are the archetypal tree for a river or lakeside. There are smaller trees and some shrubs available for the modern gardener. *Salix caprea pendula* is a deservedly popular small tree, cherished for its catkins in spring. *Salix lanata* is a shrub form, also with spring catkins. *Salix repens* and *S. reticulata* are also worth considering.

Sorbus aucuparia and varieties
The rowan, or mountain ash, is native to the UK. It will reach 15m (49ft) high, but with a spread of only 5 or 6m (16½ or 19½ft). It has white flowers in spring, and then berries which follow in late summer/autumn. The leaves also have a good autumn colour before they drop. There are a few varieties, which are useful for the different colours of their berries. *Sorbus aucuparia* 'Aspleniifolia' is featured on page 74.

Staphylea species and varieties.
These large, spring-flowering shrubs are deciduous. *Staphylea pinnata* has white flowers, *S. holocarpa* 'Rosea' has pink. The smallest have a height and spread of about 3m (10ft).

Symphoricarpos species and varieties
This genus of deciduous shrubs is most commonly seen as *Symphoricarpos albus* (snowberry). There are other types, but they are still around 2m (6½ft) in height and spread. *Symphoricarpos orbiculatus* has deep purple/red fruits. All can be pruned as a informal hedge.

Taxodium distichum (swamp cypress)
The common name is proof of this tree's need for moisture. It will reach 30m (100ft) in height and 8m (26ft) in diameter. Unusually for a conifer it is deciduous; indeed its autumn colour is one of the main reasons that it is grown in gardens. Recommended if you have the space.

Trillium species and varieties
All the trilliums make interesting garden perennials, but *Trillium grandiflorum* is outstanding for its fragrance. *Trillium sessile*, with its red/brown flowers, is always a good talking point. Some are difficult to grow and none like to be moved once established.

Trollius species and varieties (globeflowers)
These perennials flower in the spring or early summer. All are some form of yellow, although creams and oranges are now available. They

measure 90cm (30–36in) tall, except for *Trollius pumilus* which reaches 15cm (6in).

Viburnum davidii and *V. rhytidophyllum*
These are evergreen shrubs. *Viburnum davidii* grows 60cm (24in) high, with a 90cm (36in) spread; *Viburnum rhytidophyllum* has a height and spread of 3m (10ft). They are grown for their foliage, but both produce flowers and berries, too. *Viburnum davidii's* flowers are insignificant, but clumps of red berries will form if plants of both sexes are grown together. *Viburnum rhytidophyllum* has white flowers in late spring, but the dark berries are insignificant.

Viburnum opulus and varieties.
The guelder rose is a deciduous shrub native to the UK. It has good autumn colour and white flower heads in late spring/early summer. The berries are not prominent. *Viburnum opulus* 'Compactum' is featured on page 80. Other varieties are available.

Vinca species and varieties
This genus is usually represented by *Vinca minor* and *V. major*. They are very similar plants, except for their size. There are variegated forms and varieties with different coloured flowers. They are good in sun or light shade and ideal for covering old posts, stumps, and so on.

Salix caprea var. *pendula* adorned with catkins

Plants for dry soils

Even though the plants listed here are for dry areas, they still need watering until they are established. Some plants appear here and in the alkaline soil list; they are suitable for most soils. The plants in the alkaline soil list will tolerate dry soils in full sun. Plants sold as 'alpines' should also fulfil this requirement. None of the plants in this listing will like a soil that is wet during the winter. Most will make good subjects for planting in containers. Mulching is recommended in most situations.

Abelia species and varieties
Abelias are evergreen shrubs, although some types will lose their leaves in hard winters. The flowering is very good, quite unusual and tubular in shape.

Ajuga reptans and varieties
A good ground-covering perennial, *Ajuga reptans* will often stay green throughout the winter. There are excellent variegated varieties, such as 'Multicolor' and 'Burgundy Lace'. They grow best with a high level of organic matter.

Ajuga reptans 'Burgundy Lace'

Alchemilla species
The most well-known alchemilla is *Alchemilla mollis* (lady's mantle) with its yellow flowers spraying around the lovely, pale foliage. It looks very good planted in gravel or between paving stone. There are others, but they can be quite hard to find; *Alchemilla conjuncta* is smaller than *A. mollis:* 30cm (12in) as opposed to 60cm(24in).

Alyssum species and varieties
There are various alyssums and some are used as bedding. The best garden plant is *Alyssum saxatile* and its varieties. *Alyssum montanum* has fragrant flowers.

Amelanchier lamarckii
Featured on page 30.

Armeria species and varieties
A. maritima (sea thrift) is an evergreen clump of dark, grass-like foliage which bears pink flowers above in summer. The other armerias are similar. They look good by paths or rocks.

Artemisia species and varieties (wormwoods)
The wormwoods are usually perennials; some even keep their foliage through the winter. They have some of the best grey/silver foliage available to the gardener. Recommended.

Artemisia 'Powis Castle'

Aucuba species and varieties (laurels)
Laurels do best in light shade. They are evergreen shrubs grown for their foliage; their flowering is insignificant. They make excellent hedges.

Berberis species and varieties
Berberis is a huge genus of deciduous and evergreen shrubs. *Berberis thunbergii* and *B. verruculosa* are among the most popular garden plants, but most berberis are worthy of attention. See pages 32 and 31 for more on *Berberis darwinii* and *B.* × *carminea* 'Buccaneer'.

Brunnera macrophylla (Siberian bugloss)
A good, early spring-flowering perennial. It needs light shade and a good level of organic matter for best results.

Buddleja species and varieties
Deciduous shrubs (see the list of plants for alkaline soil on page 90).

Buxus sempervirens (box)
Box is a small, evergreen shrub often grown for hedging and topiary. There are various species, but you will usually be able to find *B. sempervirens*. It will reach up to 5m (16½ft) in

height and spread. *B. microphylla* is used for the very small hedges in some parks and gardens.

Caryopteris × clandonensis
A deciduous shrub with a height and spread of about 1m (3¼ft). It has blue flowers in late summer/autumn.

Ceanothus species and varieties
This is a large genus of mostly evergreen shrubs. They are sometimes grown as climbers, because many of them have foliage that needs protection from cold winter winds. The majority have blue flowers and range between 90cm (36in) and 4m (13ft) in height. *Ceanothus thyrsiflorus* var. *repens* is deservedly popular.

Ceratostigma willmottianum
This deciduous shrub has rich blue flowers in late summer/autumn. It has a height and spread of about 1m (3¼ft)

Cistus species and varieties
Evergreen shrubs (see the list for plants that like alkaline soils on page 90).

Clematis species and varieties
Clematis like good drainage, a high level of organic matter and their roots in shade. You can achieve the last by placing stones, gravel or other plants at the base of the clematis. The most well known are the large-flowered hybrids, but the species types, such as *Clematis tangutica* and *C. viticella* give extra value by forming seed head 'tassels' as well as flowers. All are climbers; most are deciduous. *Clematis alpina* is featured on page 35.

Corokia cotoneaster
Featured on page 38.

Cortaderia species and varieties (pampas grasses)
An excellent addition to any garden. Try to plant them in a sheltered position so that the plumes are not knocked down by winds.

Cotoneaster species
This large genus of deciduous and evergreen shrubs are most well known for their berries. They vary from prostrate plants to small trees. *Cotoneaster adpressus*, *C.* × *snecicus* 'Coral

Ceanothus thyrisflorus repens

Beauty', and *C.* × *snecicus* 'Skogholm' are excellent for most gardens. See page 40 for details on *Cotoneaster horizontalis*.

Clematis tangutica

Crocus species and varieties
One of the true heralds of spring. All deciduous shrubs should be under-planted with crocuses. There are some autumn-flowering crocuses as well. Note that you should purchase spring-flowering bulbs in late summer or autumn. Retailers are now offering a range of pot-grown bulbs in place of dry bulbs in packets, but there is rarely the same choice and you will pay more. See *Crocus chrysanthus* 'Cream Beauty' on page 42.

Cortaderia selloana (pampas grass)

Cytisus species (brooms)
Brooms provide some of the most spectacular spring flowers; most are yellow, but white is common, too, and red flowers have also been bred. Their fine, green branches are often devoid of leaves which gives them a delicate, wispy appearance. All are evergreen shrubs and much recommended.

Dianthus species and varieties (pinks)
Hugely popular flowers, but the foliage is often attractive as well. They have been cross-bred for decades and so a massive range of colours and flower types is available. Take care when purchasing, because not all are hardy, and some are sold as bedding plants.

Escallonia species and varieties
These excellent, evergreen shrubs make good hedges (trim after flowering) and feature plants. The summer flowering is excellent; most are pink or red.

Eschscholzia species and varieties
A genus with one of the worst names to pronounce, but some of the most superb flowers. *Eschscholzia californica* (California poppy) is a hardy annual. There have been many colours bred but they are usually only available in mixed packets, which is a shame, but you may have a suitable spot for that.

Euonymus species and varieties
All the evergreen varieties are fine for dry soils in sun or shade. (See the list of plants for alkaline soils on page 90.)

Genista species
This genus, along with cytisus, is known as 'broom'. They have long, fine, green branches, sometimes with no leaves at all. *Genista lydia* is featured on page 51. *Genista aetnensis* will reach 8–9m (26–30ft), yet provides a similar display in summer with the added bonus of fragrance. Other genistas are usually around 1m (3¼ft) tall with yellow flowers, but there are exceptions.

Grasses
Refer to the list of plants for foliage featured on page 114.

Gypsophila species and varieties
Although gypsophilas will do well in dry soils, they do need a lot of organic matter for best results. There are annual species, but the most well known are perennials. *Gypsophila paniculata* and its varieties are the most common. *Gypsophila repens* is also very good.

Hebe species and varieties
See the list of plants for foliage on page 114 and *Hebe cuppressoides* on page 52.

Hedera species and varieties
Ivies will do well in dry shade. In very dense shade, the variegated varieties may only have green leaves. See *Hedera helix* 'Glacier' on page 53.

Gypsophila repens

Helianthemum species and varieties (rock roses)
Helianthemums all flower well, but their size and foliage depends on the variety. Most are sold as alpines; not all will survive very hard winters. A light trim after they have flowered will help to keep them bushier. Evergreen.

Hibiscus species and varieties
Deciduous shrubs. For more information, see the list of plants for alkaline soils on page 90.

Hippophae rhamnoides (sea buckthorn)
A silvery, upright shrub with yellow flowers in the spring, followed by bright orange berries on the female plants (if you have a male also!). They are deciduous and will achieve a height and spread of 6m (19½ft).

Ilex species and varieties (hollies)
Hollies will grow in full sun, but they will do best in light shade. Dense shade will lessen the coloration on variegated varieties. You need male and female plants to get berries.

Iris species and varieties
Irises offer some of the most dramatic flowers in the garden. Unfortunately the foliage, although upright and interesting, is not so decorative. There are thousands and thousands of different irises, varying in size from dwarf forms at 10cm (4in) to plants of 1.2m (4ft). The small irises are often available as bulbs. Recommended, as long as organic matter is added to the soil.

Kolkwitzia amabilis 'Pink Cloud'
Featured on page 57.

Lamium species and varieties (deadnettles)
An unfortunate common name for plants that make excellent ground cover, in the right place, with good flower colour, too. *Lamium maculatum* 'Beacon Silver' is featured on page 58.

Lavandula species and varieties (lavenders)
Lavenders are hugely popular for their flowers, fragrance and herbal qualities. However, most types have pleasant foliage, too. Trim them back after they have flowered, otherwise the bushes will get very woody and lose their shape. If you want a more unusual flower, try the excellent French lavenders, *Lavandula stoechas* and its many varieties.

Lavendula stoechas is French lavender

Lavatera species and varieties (tree mallows)
Deservedly popular, summer-flowering perennials. The most common is *Lavatera olbia* 'Rosea', which is a blaze of pink flowers 1.5–2m (5–6½ft) high from early summer onwards. There are some shorter varieties being bred now. If you search, you may also find some of the more unusual species that are about 60cm (24in) tall.

Liriope species and varieties
These grassy-looking plants are evergreen and flower in late summer/autumn, depending on the variety. They are all about 30cm (12in) tall and clump forming.

Mahonia species and varieties
Mahonias will do well in dry soils, but they do need shade for best results. Most have yellow flowers in winter held above the distinctive foliage. *Mahonia* × *media* 'Charity' is particularly recommended. All are evergreen shrubs, 1.2–1.8m (4–6ft) tall.

Olearia species and varieties
Evergreen shrubs. (See the list of plants for alkaline soils on page 92.)

Pachysandra terminalis
An excellent plant for dry, dense shade. It carpets the ground with its interesting, evergreen foliage. There is also a variegated variety. Both need nurturing until they are established.

Mahonia × media 'Charity' has distinctive foliage

Perovskia atriplicifolia 'Blue Spire'
This upright, deciduous shrub is quite unusual. It has finely cut, grey/green foliage and violet flowers in late summer to autumn. It reaches a height of 1.2m (4ft).

Phlomis fruticosa (Jerusalem sage)
An interesting grey/green, evergreen shrub with yellow flowers in late spring to early summer. It will reach a maximum of only 1m (3¼ft) in height, but will spread to 1.5m (5ft).

Phormium species and varieties
Phormiums are evergreen, tropical-looking plants. The upright foliage can be easily damaged by wind. There are excellent bronze-coloured and variegated varieties. *Phormium tenax* 'Purpureum' is featured on page 65.

Phygelius species and varieties
Phygelius do not like to be very dry, but a copious quantity of organic matter will prevent problems. They are grown for their superb, tubular flowers. They are evergreen, but will die back in colder areas or harsh winters. When this happens, cut back to the live wood and they will grow back again.

Potentilla species and varieties
Deciduous shrubs, and perennials. See the list of plants for alkaline soils on page 93 and *Potentilla fruticosa* 'Elizabeth' on page 68.

Prunus laurocerasus and varieties
An evergreen shrub that grows low, but wide, and has white flowers in spring. The varieties 'Otto Luyken' and 'Zabeliana' are more common, because of better flowering, particularly the latter.

Prunus tenella 'Fire Hill'
This deciduous shrub will reach up to 2m (6½ft) in height. It gives a spectacular spring show of deep pink flowers.

Pulmonaria species and varieties
Early spring-flowering perennials, excellent for shade, with a wide range of flower colours available. They are susceptible to **mildew**, but are otherwise recommended.

Pulmonaria saccharata 'White Barn'

Ribes species and varieties
The flowering currants are superb spring-flowering plants. *Ribes odoratum* is featured on page 72. See also the list of berrying plants featured on page 100.

Romneya species and varieties
Romneya coulteri is another plant known by the common name of California poppy (the other being *Eschscholzia california*). It has delightful grey foliage, but its best feature is the fragrant white flowers in summer. Perennial, it is often found represented by the variety 'White Cloud', which at up to 1m (3¼ft)) is taller and more woody than the species.

Rosmarinus species and varieties
This genus comprises evergreen shrubs. *Rosmarinus officinalis* is the herb known as 'rosemary'. A light prune each spring will retain bushiness.

Rubus species and varieties
Rubus will live happily in dry soils, spreading (slowly) by pushing roots through the soil. They vary from small, ground-cover plants to the dramatic, arching branches of *Rubus* × tridel 'Benenden'.

Salvia officinalis and varieties
Not the plants commonly seen as bedding, but the herb known as 'Sage'. Variegated and tri-colour foliage plants are available.

Santolina species and varieties
A genus of small shrubs. Of particular note are *Santolina virens* with glossy green, heather-like foliage and yellow flowers, and *S. chamaecyparissus* with grey/silver foliage, and yellow flowers, both up to 45cm (18in) tall.

Santolina chamaecyparissus

Sedum species and varieties
In this genus is a hugely varied range of annuals and perennials. Sedums have been cross-bred extensively and many colours are available. The largest range of sedums will be found in the alpine plant section, but there are some perennials that are larger and good for mixed borders.

Skimmia species and varieties
Small, evergreen shrubs requiring shade. See the list of plants for acid soils on page 88.

Spartium junceum
An evergreen shrub. See the list of plants for alkaline soils on page 93.

Spiraea species and varieties
Deciduous shrubs. See the list of plants for alkaline soils on page 93 and *Spiraea* × *bumalda* 'Goldmound' on page 76.

Symphoricarpos species and varieties
This genus is mostly grown for its white 'snowberries', a range of deciduous shrubs about 1.5m (5ft) tall.

Tamarix species and varieties
Deciduous shrubs. See the plants for alkaline soils on page 94.

Thymus species and varieties (thymes)
Thymes are important for their herbal qualities, but there are numerous varieties available for their ornamental value, too. They are usually found in the alpine plant section at a garden centre.

Tulipa species and varieties
Tulips will often naturalize in a well-drained, sunny site.

Vinca species and varieties
Good, evergreen, ground-cover plants. See the list of plants for alkaline soils on page 94.

Waldsteinia ternata
Forms a prostrate, glossy green mat with yellow flowers on spikes held above in spring.

Yucca species and varieties
Yuccas are well known as houseplants, but there are some reliable hardy types. *Yucca filamentosa* and *Y. flaccida* are the hardiest. *Yucca gloriosa* and *Y. whipplei* will be fine in warmer areas or sheltered positions. The latter has superb flowering. Yuccas are really grown for their tropical-like foliage, but they will all flower too. Give them full sun.

Plants for foliage

Here is a list of plants which will make a good feature even without flowers or some other seasonal feature. Some still do have good flowering, however. The majority are evergreen, but there are a few exceptions, where the foliage or shape is of particular interest. It should also be noted that many flowering plants have a variegated foliage form available.

Acer palmatum and *A. japonicum* varieties (Japanese maples)
The Japanese maples provide some of the most outstanding foliage and forms in gardening. Many, many varieties are available; most have good autumn colour; all are deciduous. Check ultimate height and spread before you buy, because they do vary. *Acer palmatum* 'Dissectum' is featured on page 28.

Acer platanoides 'Drummondii'
One of the most well-known variegated trees, this plant's only real weakness is its tendency to produce branches with all-green leaves. These should be removed, because they are more vigorous than the variegated foliage and will gradually take over. It needs a soil with a high level of organic matter and will reach a maximum height of about 12m (40ft) with a slightly narrower spread.

Actinidia kolomikta
This interesting climber with its striking variegation needs full sun in order to achieve the best results. Half of most of the leaves turn pink and white. For more details and a photo see page 10.

Artemisia species and varieties
A lot of artemisia varieties have silver/grey foliage; the species are usually green. They are usually small shrubs/perennials. Some are evergreen, including *Artemisia* 'Powis Castle'.

Chamaecyparis lawsoniana varieties
Probably the most varied single species in gardening, there are lawsoniana varieties ranging in height from a few centimetres to large shrubs or small trees. There are golden, blue and variegated forms, including one of the most popular conifers in the UK, *Chamaecyparis lawsoniana* 'Ellwoodii'. Be aware that some plants sold as dwarf are in fact just slow growing and will turn into tree-sized plants in time. All are evergreen.

Chamaecyparis pisifera 'Boulevard'
A slow-growing, evergreen conifer with lovely, steel-blue foliage. It will eventually reach a height of 1.2m (4ft). Partial shade is best, but it will grow in full sun. A good subject for container growing. When purchasing, try to pick a plant with foliage to the base; if it is absent it is unlikely to grow back again and this may spoil the desired pyramidal shape in years to come.

Choisya ternata 'Sundance'
This is a superb, golden, evergreen shrub which reaches 2m (6½ft) in height and spread. It likes partial shade. See page 34 for more details.

Corylus avellana 'Contorta'
Featured on page 39.

Cryptomeria japonica and varieties
The feathery foliage of these evergreen conifers is a delight, especially with the varieties that turn red in the autumn and winter. Dwarf and larger forms are available. *Cryptomeria japonica* 'Elegans' is featured on page 43.

Elaeagnus species and varieties
A range of evergreen shrubs best known for its variegated forms, such as *Elaeagnus × ebbingei* 'Limelight'. Most have a height and spread of 2m (6½ft). *Elaeagnus × ebbingei* is a fast-growing, blue plant which makes an excellent hedge. *Elaeagnus pungens* 'Maculata' is featured on page 45.

Eucalyptus species
All eucalyptus have grey foliage, but particularly recommended is *Eucalyptus gunnii*. This is because the leaves are smaller, and more rounded that most and it makes an excellent shrub if pruned hard every few years. It can also make a nice, small tree, though the larger-leafed varieties, such as *Eucalyptus niphophila*, are better for that.

Eucalyptus gunnii

Euonymus fortunei varieties
There is a wide range of plants within this species, but it is deservedly well known for the two varieties 'Emerald Gaiety', a white/green variegation, providing ground cover, which grows to about 0.5m (1½ft) high, and 'Emerald Gold' – similar, but with golden coloration.

Euphorbia species and varieties
A exciting range of perennials which usually have interesting foliage. The bracts/flowers are an excellent bonus. Be aware that the sap is often an irritant, especially if it comes into contact with the eyes.

Grasses
Ornamental grasses are grown for their flowers and seed heads, but they are often worth growing just for their general appearance. Most form clumps of wiry foliage and some can be treated as evergreen. Stipa and miscanthus are useful genera as ornamental grasses. *Miscanthus sinensis* 'Zebrinus' is featured on page 60. *Festuca glauca* and its varieties are also interesting. Grasses here include bamboos, and cortaderias (pampas grass), of which there are a few varieties, including a golden form.

Heathers
Heathers are plants in the Erica, Calluna and Daboecia genera. They are really grown for their flowers, but some varieties, particularly ericas, have very good foliage, too. There are excellent golden forms, and many interesting shades of green, all growing in the distinctive clump style of a heather. For more information, see the entry for heathers in the Glossary, and *Erica* × *darleyensis* on page 46.

Hebe species and varieties
Most hebes form lovely rounded mounds and their flowering is an added bonus. There are coppery-coloured, variegated and golden-foliage hebes. When purchasing, find out if they are hardy, because some are not and are used as summer bedding plants. All hebes need good drainage to survive the winter. They make good container plants, but take note of the final size of the type before you purchase. *Hebe cuppressoides* is featured on page 52. Also

Euphorbia palustris (orange) and *Euphorbia griffithii* 'Fireglow' (yellow)

recommended are *Hebe buxifolia*, *H. albicans*, *H. ochracea* and *H. rakaiensis*.

Hedera species and varieties
Ivies are very useful, evergreen climbers. There is a wide range of sizes growing to a height of 2–6m (6½–19½ft). There are some superb golden and white variegated forms. *Hedera helix* 'Goldheart' is deservedly popular; *H. helix* 'Glacier' is a good white variegation (see page 53). For larger plants, *Hedera colchica* varieties are recommended.

Hedera colchica

Parthenocissus tricuspidata

Hosta species and varieties
A huge genus usually grown for its foliage, although they do flower in summer. All hostas prefer some sort of shade, although some of the all-green varieties will grow in full sun. They all like a moist soil, with a good level of organic matter, but they still make good container subjects. They are perennials and therefore deciduous. Highly recommended.

Ilex species and varieties
There are some excellent variegated and blue hollies. If the latter intrigues you, look for *Ilex* × *meserveae* varieties such as Blue Princess. If it is berries you want, make sure you get a male and a female plant. Do not rely on names to distinguish between the sexes; for example, *Ilex* × *altclerensis* 'Golden King' is female. All are evergreen and can be clipped as a hedge or for topiary.

Juniperus species and varieties
Junipers are a sort of conifer. There are thousands of different varieties, varying from dwarf and prostrate plants to full-sized trees. The ground-cover varieties, such as *Juniperus horizontalis* 'Emerald Spreader', are well worth investigating. There are variegated and golden forms available in most shapes and sizes. All are evergreen. *Juniperus squamata* 'Blue Star' is featured on page 56.

Parthenocissus species and varieties
An excellent genus of climbers. Although some have interesting foliage in the summer – *Parthenocissus henryana*, for example – but the outstanding reason for growing these plants is the autumn colour, particularly of that *P. tricuspidata* and its varieties.

Phormium species and varieties
The tropical-looking phormiums need shelter in the winter, because they are evergreen and the upright foliage can be badly damaged by wind. There are excellent bronze-coloured and variegated varieties. Good for container growing. See *Phormium tenax* 'Purpureum' on page 65.

Rosa rubrifolia
Yes, a rose being recommended for its foliage! This deciduous plant looks most unusual during spring/summer when, in its short flowering season, the pink flowers complement the dark red stems and the grey-purple foliage.

Tamarix species
Tamarisks are large, feathery-looking shrubs up to 3.5m (11½ft) tall. They all have pink flowers in late summer. Recommended if you have the room and an alkaline soil.

Thuja species and varieties
The soft foliage of these evergreen conifers is quite unusual compared to most conifers. This genus contains mostly smaller-growing plants, although some varieties are several metres tall. *Thuja plicata* 'Atrovirens' is an excellent hedge plant that can be pruned to 1.5–3m (5–10ft) and is a lovely, rich green. This genus also contains my favourite golden plant, *Thuja occidentalis* 'Rheingold', which turns more coppery

coloured in the autumn/winter. See *Thuja occidentalis* 'Smaragd" on page 78.

Tsuga species and varieties
Among the hemlocks there are some very elegant plants. Their needles are softer than most conifers and this lends them a more feathery appearance. The species are usually trees, but smaller varieties are available, such as *Tsuga canadensis* 'Jeddeloh', which is featured on page 79. All are evergreen.

Thuja occidentalis 'Rheingold'

Plants for interesting bark or twigs

Here are plants mainly for winter interest, although on older plants the bark can be admired all year round. Trees need to be pruned as **standards** for this, that is, with a length of bare trunk, if they do not naturally drop their lower branches as they age. Please note that some effects, particularly stylized bark, may not be apparent for the first few years in a plant's life. It may well be worth looking at some bamboos too, mainly arundinaria, phyllostachys and sasa. Also remember that some plants have young growth which may also be attractive or interesting. As with other features, you should consider how the bark or twigs of a plant will contrast with or complement the foliage or flower colour of adjacent plants.

Acer capillipes (one of the snake-bark maples)
The common name gives you an idea of what to expect. Good autumn colour on an excellent small tree.

Acer davidii
A small tree with interesting striped bark on older specimens and good autumn colour.

Acer griseum
Featured on page 26.

Acer grosseri var. *hersii*
A superb small tree, with striped bark, good autumn colour and interesting young foliage.

Acer henryi
A small tree with deep green bark and interesting young foliage.

Acer palmatum 'Senkaki'
A slow-growing large shrub or small tree on which the golden autumn colour gives way to coral-red stems.

Betula albosinensis var. *septentrionalis*
A small to medium birch tree with pinkish-red bark.

Betula jacquemontii
Probably the best birch tree for the whiteness of

Acer grosseri hersii has striking striped bark

its bark. It only creates light shade, and makes an excellent choice for all but the smallest gardens.

Betula papyrifera
A large, elegant tree. Similar to the UK's native birch, except that the bark is not white and peels in thin 'ruffs'.

Betula pendula 'Tristis'
A smaller-growing form of the UK's native birch tree with graceful, twisted branches.

Betula pendula 'Youngii'

Betula pendula 'Youngii'
Probably one of the most common trees in the suburbs of the UK, this small, weeping tree is deservedly popular. Best left unpruned; it can be trained to a height of 2–4m (6½–13ft). The white of the trunk and main branches only really occurs on older plants and is hidden by the foliage. It looks good throughout the winter months.

Cornus alba and varieties
Mostly grown for their red, winter bark colour. Try to pick a variety with other features, such as variegated leaves. *Cornus alba* 'Elegantissima' is excellent. Size depends on the variety, but they are usually about 1.5m (5ft) high and wide. Prune out older wood regularly to keep the good winter colour.

Cornus stolonifera 'Flaviramea'
This has yellow branches in the winter and looks good with the red-twigged dogwoods, but is otherwise uninteresting. Will grow to 2m (6½ft) in height and spread, but is best pruned each spring.

Corokia cotoneaster
Featured on page 38.

Corylus avellana 'Contorta'
Featured on page 39.

Corylus colurna (Turkish hazel)
This will eventually become a large tree. The bark looks like cork when it is young and will then start to flake. Yellow catkins in Feb/March.

Eleagnus × ebbingei
The young growth on good forms of this plant looks like it is covered with silver fur, but the plant is always interesting. A large shrub that is good for hedging.

Fraxinus excelsior 'Aurea Pendula'
Foliage is yellow in spring and green in summer. The bark is also yellow and looks wonderful in winter sunshine.

Genista lydia
Has arching branches which form a hummock and provide year-round interest, the mass of bright yellow flowers in May being a superb bonus. Featured on page 51.

Kerria japonica
The double-flowering and variegated forms are more common, but the arching branches make this an elegant shrub. Grows to 1.8m (6ft), but its spread is always a little narrower.

Leycesteria formosa
An elegant shrub with stems that are quite like bamboo and crimson when young, as are the new leaves. Flowers well in mid- to late summer. Grows to 1.8m (6ft) high, but its spread is slightly narrower.

Nandina domestica 'Firepower'
Featured on page 61.

Poncirus trifoliata
This large shrub looks like it has been moulded from green plastic! It makes a good barrier plant, because it has rather large thorns.

Prunus 'Kanzan'
Famous for its brilliant display of pink flowers in spring, this wide-spreading tree also gets a deep sheen to its bark, especially if it is rubbed regularly. The narrower *Prunus* 'Shirofugen' is featured on page 69.

Prunus serrula
A small to medium tree with deep mahogany-coloured bark which peels, and white flowers in May.

Robinia pseudoacacia 'Frisia'
This small tree is usually grown for its lovely foliage. However, its rich brown bark, with its sharp inch-long spines, make it interesting during all seasons.

Rubus cockburnianus
A plant for the more informal garden; a dramatic sight of arching, white branches up to 2.5m (8ft) high and almost as wide.

Salix alba 'Chermesina'
A small willow tree whose youngest branches are bright scarlet. Prune older wood occasionally (in spring) to keep the best winter colour. Can be kept as a large shrub.

Salix matsudana 'Tortuosa' (dragon's-claw willow)
A narrow-growing tree, which looks good most of the year, but is best in winter. Will eventually grow to 15m (49ft).

The bare white branches of *Rubus biflorus* 'Quinqueflorus' look almost ghostly

Plants for winter flowers

These plants provide welcome colour in the garden throughout winter. You should also refer to the list of berrying plants which begins on page 99.

Alnus incana 'Aurea'
All alder trees have catkins over winter or early spring, but this tree is particularly striking.

Camellia
Evergreen shrubs with flowers ranging from red to pink and through to white. They like an acid soil, but shouldn't be planted in a position where early morning sun pitches onto frost-covered buds, because that will destroy them, preventing flowering.

Chimonanthus praecox
A shrub requiring a sheltered site. The flowers can be cut for indoor display.

Chionodoxa
Early-flowering bulbs, in pink or blue.

Clematis balecaria
A climber with ivory flowers.

Cornus mas
A large shrub with white flowers.

Corylus avellana 'Contorta' (contorted hazel)
Provides a good show of catkins. Featured on page 39.

Crocus
Crocuses flower from January to March and are available in a wide range of colours. The flowers can be damaged by rain. *Crocus* 'Cream Beauty' is featured on page 42.

Cyclamen
A few varieties of cyclamen are hardy and some of them flower in late autumn/winter. Particularly good is the variety *Cyclamen coum coum.*

Daphne mezereum
Produces purple to red, scented flowers on bare stems.

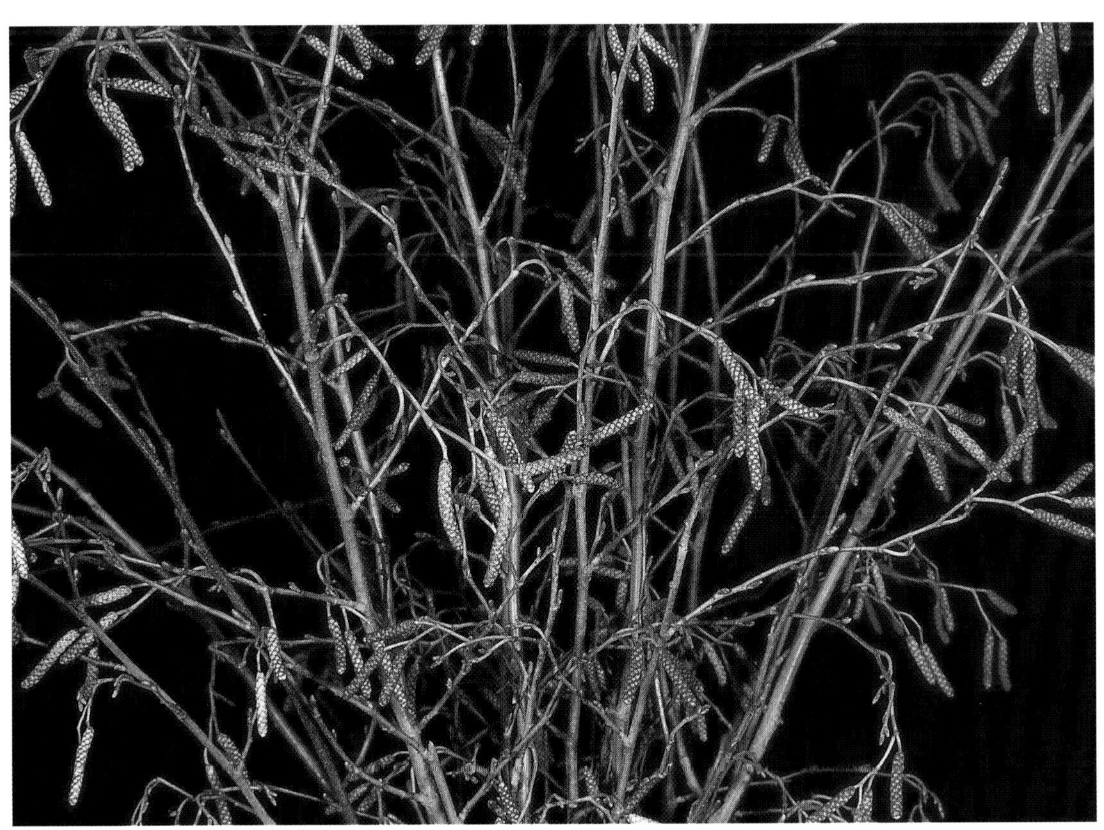

Alnus incana 'Aurea'

Cyclamen hederifolium album

Elaeagnus × *ebbingei*
A large, blue shrub with scented, but otherwise insignificant, flowers.

Eranthis hyemalis (winter aconite)
Requires moist soil and prefers shade (ie. native of woodlands). Good for planting underneath trees and shrubs that like similar conditions.

Erica (heathers)
Many different varieties. Some are not winter flowering.

Galanthus (snowdrops)
There are a few varieties, but they all have white flowers. *Galanthus nivalis* is featured on page 50.

Garraya elliptica
Evergreen shrub, best trained against a wall. Superb catkin display in February/March.

Hamamelis
Large shrubs with (usually) yellow, scented flowers. *Hamamelis* × *intermedia* 'Jelena' has orange flowers and excellent autumn colour, too. Recomended plants for acid soil.

Helleborus
Look for *Helleborus niger* (Christmas rose) or *orientalis* varieties. These are perennials that needs a moist, shady spot for best results.

Iris
Iris reticulata and its varieties flower in late winter to early spring. Various colours available.

Jasminum nudiflorum (winter jasmine)
Derservedly one of our most popular shrubs. Flowers best if trained against wall or fence. Branches will root readily if they are touching the ground.

Helleborus orientalis

Mahonia × 'Charity'
An excellent evergreen shrub, with good structural qualities. The other mahonias are also good for winter flowers, except *Mahonia aquifolium.*

Narcissus
Comes in a wide range of flowers, mostly variations of yellow and white. Most will flower into early spring. *Narcissus* 'Tete-a-Tete' is featured on page 62.

Parrotia persica
This tree bears red flowers from January to March and will also give good autumn colour. It needs good soil.

Primula
Some primulas and polyanthus will flower in late winter.

Prunus × *subhirtella* 'Autumnalis'
A small tree with pale pink flowers. *Prunus* × *subhirtella* 'Autumnalis Rosea' is even more pink.

Sarcococca
Various evergreen shrubs all bearing small but fragrant cream-white flowers, although some varieties appear pink. The flowers are followed by berries.

Viburnum × *bodnantense*
Delicate pink flowers on bare stems.

Viburnum farreri
A large shrub that bears scented, white or pale pink flowers.

Viburnum tinus
An evergreen that flowers reliably and is good for hedging. Some varieties available.

If you must have roses...

Roses will always create work in the garden. The old, shrub rose varieties and species roses are much less prone to pests and diseases than the modern hybrids, but they tend to have a much shorter flowering period. In recent years, rose breeders have been producing roses with much better resistance to the common problems of black spot, green fly and mildew. As a general rule, if you have the information, avoid hybrids from the 1950s to 1980s. A regular programme of spraying (fortnightly) and feeding will keep roses in good health.

As with most flowering plants, a general or flowering plant fertilizer is recommended (eg.Vitax Q4). It should be first applied in early April for growth, and again in mid-June/July for the flowers. Any dead wood should be pruned out and burnt or binned. The same applies when you prune your roses back in the winter.

Hybrid tea roses are the classic flower that everyone thinks of and are the most work. Floribundas are similar, but their flowers tend to be less showy. Unlike the hybrid teas, they will flower right through the summer. Climbing roses will also flower all summer, but they must not be confused with rambling roses. Ramblers may have a second flush of flowers, but usually only flower once each year and they will get a lot bigger than climbers. Being older plants, ramblers have a good resistance to disease. Climbers will need pruning; ramblers just need controlling from time to time.

There are various types of shrub rose, the distinctions being based on the parentage. All have good resistance to disease and need little attention. Of particular note for the aims of this book are the 'New English' shrub roses bred by David Austin. These have a long flowering period and are tidy plants with good resistance to disease. If you want to maximize the display in a limited space, choose a variety that will have rose **hips**; some are quite dramatic. *Rosa rugosa* varieties are the most well known for hips. See also *Rosa moyesii* 'Geranium' featured on page 73.

Shrub rose

Also available are patio or miniature roses. As you may guess, they have been bred for the modern, smaller garden and will even be happy in pots (normal roses are not). They flower for a long time and are easy to look after.

This leaves the ground-cover or landscape roses. These plants often hark back to the wilder appearance of the old shrub roses, but usually grow less tall. They also tend to have a much longer flowering period. If you have the space, any rose described as 'ground cover' will be an easy, showy specimen which should not need much attention. For most gardens, however, of particular note are the 'County' series of roses by Mattocks Roses. *Rosa* Gwent is mentioned in the listing here, but there are numerous other 'counties' available, mostly with white or pink flowers. They do vary in height from about 30cm (12in) to 1m (3¼ft), with a spread of up to 2m (6½ft), depending on the variety. I find that there is very little maintenance with either of these two in my garden; the main job is to remove the longer branches which occasionally shoot out from the main body of the plant.

Rosa Gwent

Easy roses for maximum show

Rosa 'Dunwich Rose'
An early-flowering (white), shrub-type rose. It doesn't flower for long, but it is very easy to look after and has more interesting foliage and habit than most roses. Will spread by suckers.

Rosa Flower Carpet™
A modern marketing phenomenon. It received a great deal of hype in 1997/98 and is in fact a very good ground-cover rose. It grows to a height of 60cm (24in) and has pink flowers.

Rosa 'Fru Dagmar Hastrup'
This would be a superb plant except that, in my experience, it has a tendency to produce weak branches. It is a shrub-type plant bearing pink/purple flowers most of the summer and hips in the autumn.

Rosa Gertrude Jekyll®
A New English shrub-type rose with pink, fragrant flowers, growing to about 1.5m (5ft) in height. A superb rose, named after one of the most famous gardeners this century.

Rosa Graham Thomas
A New English shrub-type, growing to 1.5m (5ft) with fragrant, yellow flowers.

Rosa Gwent
A ground-cover rose growing to about 45cm (18in) with flowers that are yellow fading to white. One of my favourite plants. See picture opposite.

Rosa Kent®
A delightful ground-cover rose, about 90cm (36in) tall with white flowers.

Rosa 'Max Graf'
A ground-cover rose with pink flowers. Reaches a height of 1m (3¼ft) and will spread wide.

Rosa moyesii 'Geranium'
A superb plant with fine-leafed foliage, dark red flowers in early summer and hips in the autumn. See page 73.

Rosa chinensis 'Mutabilis'
A shrub rose reaching 1.5m (5ft) in height with dark yellow flowers that often last right up until Christmas.

Rosa 'Nevada'
A white-flowering shrub rose, about 2m (6½ft) tall. Will not flower continuously, but has reliable extra flushes in late summer. The almost complete lack of thorns helps with aftercare!

Rosa rubrifolia
A shrub rose with excellent foliage and few pest and disease problems. Bears pink flowers for a short while in early summer and hips in autumn. Will grow up to 2m (6½ft) tall.

Rosa 'Roseraie de l'Haÿ'
Bears fragrant, double, crimson flowers for most of the summer then some hips in autumn. A shrub rose reaching a height of 2m (6½ft).

Rosa Surrey
A ground-cover rose, about 75cm (30in) tall, with pink flowers.

Rosa The Seckford Rose
A modern hybrid rose with fragrant, double pink flowers. It usually has a good shape and foliage and will grow to 1.5m (5ft).

Rosa xanthina 'Canarybird'
A 2m (6½ft) tall shrub rose with yellow flowers. It does not flower for long, but will be the first rose out in your garden and is easy to grow.

GLOSSARY

Aeration
Soil contains air and it is vital to successful plant growth. Aeration is the improvement of soil by means of digging, aerating with hollow tines or by adding organic matter.

Alpines
Strictly speaking, this means a plant which naturally grows in the Alps. It has come to mean any plant that is compact in size and will grow in a rockery-type environment, that is, in well-drained soil in full sun.

Annual
A plant which completes its life-cycle in one year. The seed is sown in the winter or spring, it germinates, and grows and flowers that summer. It then drops its seed (or it is collected) in the late summer/autumn. Hardy annuals are useful for bursts of easy-to-grow colour.

Bare root
Used to describe a plant whose roots have no soil or compost around them. This is because it has been grown in a field, rather than a container, and has been dug up for sale. The plants will be supplied with some packing material (usually straw) in a bag. They will die if the roots dry out.

Bedding plants
Plants that are grown for one year – such as nicotiana, marigolds, busy lizzies (impatiens) and geraniums – the main reason being that they are not hardy. Some can over-winter in a greenhouse or conservatory, but a lot have expended so much of their energy producing flowers that they are not worth keeping. Some are also annuals.

Bonemeal
A powder made from animal bones. It is a good fertilizer for root growth, so it is often used at the planting stage. In spring, fish, blood and bone can be used to feed the rest of the plant.

Border
Another word for a flower bed which evolved because flower beds were usually around the edge or border of a garden.

Bracts
A specialized leaf which, as far as the gardener is concerned, can be treated like a flower. Good examples are to be seen on euphorbias and poinsettias.

Bulbs
Plants such as daffodils, tulips, snowdrops and lilies. These plants are perennial, dying down to the bulb each year after flowering. The bulb is basically a specialized storage organ that holds the food the plant needs over the winter and which will be needed for regrowth the following year. There are many available, but not all are hardy. Non-hardy bulbs should be taken out of the ground each autumn and stored somewhere free of frost during the winter. Dahlias are the most popular example of tender bulbs.

Columnar
A plant that grows in the shape of a column, a fact that may not always be obvious when the plant is very young.

Common name
The name in spoken language for a plant or plants. Common names vary tremendously even for the same plant, which is why horticulturists, botanists and other scientists use Latin, or scientfic, naming.

Conifers
Plants such as junipers, leylandii, fir and pine, which have needles or fronds rather than leaves, and bear their seeds in cones. With very few exceptions, they are evergreen.

Cultural methods

The way one cultures one's plants or how one gardens. Cultural methods are usually referred to in the context of controlling pest problems, especially by gardeners who do not want to use chemicals. For instance, a cultural method for controlling slugs is to go out in the dark with a torch and pick them up.

Deciduous
A plant which loses its leaves annually at the end of the growing season.

Double digging
The length of the blade of a spade is called a spit and we normally dig to the depth of one spit. Double digging is for serious, long-term improvement of the soil and is done by digging down two spits and adding organic matter.

Ericaceous
This is used to describe plants which need a soil with an acid pH (less than 7).

Established
Used to describe a plant whose roots have had time to spread into the surrounding soil in search of food and water and can now be left to its own devices. A year (one growing season) is usually enough.

Evergreen
A plant which keeps its leaves or foliage all year round.

Fastigiate
A plant which grows in a narrow, upright fashion. The most common examples of this are poplar trees, *Juniperus* 'Skyrocket' and *Prunus* 'Amanogawa'.

Fertilizer
Plant food. A general fertilizer might be *Growmore* or fish, blood and bone. There are numerous other branded general fertilisers, such as *Vitax Q4*, *Miracle-gro* and *Phostrogen*. These are good for short-term boosts to plant growth, at flowering time, for instance, but cannot replace having the correct soil and light in the first place. The other sort of fertilizer is for specific requirements: Epsom salts to correct magnesium deficiency in the soil, for example.

Field grown
See Bare root.

Foliage
Leaves etc.

Genus
A grouping of closely related species (plants in this case), even though they may not look alike.

Ground cover
This description refers to a plant which, with its propensity for growing close to the ground and its dense foliage, blocks out the light and thereby discourages weeds.

Habit
The style in which a plant grows. An open plant is one whose branches are wide apart; in a dense plant they are tight together. It also refers to the shape a plant takes, such as fastigiate (see the entry above).

Hard landscape
The parts of a garden that are 'hard', such as paths and paving, arches, pergolas and statues.

Hardiness
The degree of hardiness of a plant determines how likely it is going to survive a winter outside without protection. A plant that is fully hardy needs no protection.

Hardy
See Hardiness.

Heathers
A common name for erica, daboecia and calluna. Calluna is the UK's native heather, as seen on moorlands. Callunas and daboecias need an acid soil, as do some ericas. Ericas are the most useful in the garden, because they will grow in most soils and there are varieties for flowering at any season of the year. *Erica carnea* and *Erica* × *darleyensis* varieties can be grown in most soils, including lime.

Herbaceous perennial
A plant whose leaves and stems die down each autumn and return in the spring. Most appreciate a mulch once their foliage has gone.

Hip
A brightly coloured, berry-like swollen receptacle containing the fruits of a rose.

Horticulture
The science of understanding or caring for plants. Gardening is one part of it and an area in which the professional and amateur overlap far more than in any other area of knowledge, to the benefit of both parties, I believe.

Hybrid
See Variety.

Invasive
A plant that is invasive will grow indefinitely and often aggressively, swamping other plants around it. A good example in the countryside is the bramble. They are only a problem in the garden if planted in the wrong place, but the problem is often associated with some of the bamboos and quite a few spreading perennials, such as lamium.

Leaf scorch
Burnt foliage often caused because the plant is in an area that is too bright for it, but also by chemicals. Roadside plants suffer from the latter as do plants tended by gardeners who 'add a little bit extra to make sure' when applying pesticides.

Loam
Rich soil consisting of a mixture of sand, clay and decaying organic matter. It is moisture-retentive but free-draining.

Mildew
Various diseases of plants that affect mainly the leaves and are caused by a parasitic fungi.

Mulch
A covering over the surface of the soil, usually of bark or tree shreddings. Cocoa shell is very good, because it feeds the plants a little and repels slugs. You can also use a landscape fabric.

Naturalize
A non-native plant can fit so well into a foreign country or place that it propagates itself and generally acts as if it belongs there. A good example is the sycamore tree (*Acer platanoides*), introduced to the UK by the Romans. Daffodils often naturalize in lawns if they are mown correctly.

Perennial
A plant that dies down each autumn and grows again in the spring from the same roots. Perennials are not necessarily hardy – the Venus flytrap houseplant, for example – but those that aren't make more work. Perennials will live for a number of years – at least three – and most for an indefinite period.

Pests and diseases
Pests are insects and other animals (including humans!) that harm your plants. If the problem is slight, it is easier to live with it than tackle it. Various pesticides are available to assist the modern gardener, but cultural techniques can be used to control the problem. Plant diseases are not normally treatable; the best way of dealing with them is to prune out the infected tissue. As with animals, the best way to avoid health problems is to put the plant in the right conditions and feed it correctly.

Pot-bound
A plant that has been in its container so long that its roots have spiralled round and round, forming a dense mat. This is harmful to the plant and may not be remedied by simply planting it out in the garden, so avoid buying plants in this condition. If the plant is in a pot permanently, it will be harder to keep the compost moist; it really needs a larger pot.

Potting compost
A medium that is used instead of soil when growing plants in pots and other containers. It has qualities which aid aeration, drainage and food retention that your garden soil is unlikely to possess.

Propagation
The making of more plants from a parent. It usually refers to techniques used by people such as cuttings, grafting and layering.

Prostrate
A plant whose branches or foliage grow very

close to the ground. Prostrate plants are normally quite dense as well and thus make good ground cover.

Prune
The removal of a selected piece of plant. The main reasons for doing this are to remove dead or diseased wood, or to reshape the plant. Pruning is a selective process, unlike trimming a hedge which is just cutting.

Root-wrapped
A bare-root plant whose roots have been put in some form of container for transportation or protection. Lilacs are often sold in this way, as are daphnes and hedging plants.

Shrub
A woody plant. Shrubs vary considerably in size and shape. A large shrub can be a small tree and vice versa, although the shrub is likely to be branched from the base whereas the tree will have a single bare stem before the branches.

Soft landscape
The soft landscape is the living part of the garden: the plants and soil.

Species
The species defines the particular plant within a genus. The genus and species names combined specify which plant is being discussed. Individual plants may vary within a species. The species name usually means something, e.g. alba means white, floribunda means lots of flowers, wilsonae is named after someone called Wilson, and so on. A few plants may have an 'x' before the species name; this indicates that two different plants were cross-bred to make the new species.

Specimen plant
This usually refers to a plant you can purchase at a larger than normal size. They are very useful for instant effect in your garden and worth putting into a prime spot, or if you are impatient!

Spit
The height of the blade of a spade. With sufficient effort, the hole you dig is likely to be one spit deep.

Spread
The width of a plant, taken as a diameter of a circle. If you are planting a group of the same plant, you should put them slightly less than this distance apart, closer if you want the plants to grow together quicker.

Standard
A tree with at least 2m (6ft) of stem below the first branches, or a shrub trained so that it has a clear length of stem below the branches: 1–1.2m (3–4ft) for roses.

Tender
If a plant is tender, it will be severely damaged or killed by low temperatures or frost. This covers houseplants (it is why they are in the house), bedding plants and some perennials and shrubs.

Topiary
A specialized form of pruning in which the gardener makes a shape with the plant. Animals are common, but anything goes these days.

Trace elements
Nutrients that a plant needs in very small amounts, such as the minerals magnesium and iron. If a plant is deficient in any particular element, the foliage or flowers will display distinctive symptoms. Nutrient deficiencies are unusual in ornamental plants.

Variegation
Leaves are variegated if they are mottled in more than one colour. The usual combination is white and green, the white often being around the edge of the leaf. Yellow is also common with green, but other, more unusual plants are available with multicoloured foliage or no green at all.

Variety
Every plant has a Latin name, but some have been selectively bred and these are called varieties. In print they can be distinguished by the inverted commas that enclose the name of the variety after the italic species name – for example, *Garrya elliptica* 'James Roof' or *Solanum crispum* 'Glasnevin'. A few may have an 'x' before the species name; this indicates that two different plants were cross-bred to make the new species.

FURTHER INFORMATION

Further Reading

There are many gardening magazines available. Particularly good for guidance and advice are *Gardeners' World*, *Garden Answers* and *Practical Gardening* and GMC's *Water Gardening* and *Exotic Gardening*.

Hessayon, Dr D.G., *Expert Books* series
Deservedly one of the world's best-selling authors on a whole range of plants and gardening. Unbeatable value for money and with more accurate information than most.

RHS Gardeners' Encyclopaedia of Plants and Flowers, Dorling Kindersley
I can't recommend this book highly enough.

Which Gardening
Pretty good, if you like the Which style of advice. Do take some of their recommendations with a pinch of salt, such as the idea that fertilizer is a waste of money and, in my opinion, their trials are not very scientific.

Fleming, Laurence, *The One-Hour Garden*, Ward Lock Ltd
A bit odd, because it is for such easy gardening that I am not sure it really counts as gardening! Some strange plant recommendations too, but some useful ideas.

Ferguson, Nicola, *Right Plant, Right Place*
Has lists of plants for different places in the garden.

RHS Plant Finder, Dorling Kindersley
Worth purchasing if you would like to have a wide range of plants and want to avoid just buying the common ones. It lists all the plants known by the RHS to be available commercially in the UK and who sells them. It is very useful for eliminating one of my pet irritations: finding just the plant you want in a gardening book and not being able to find where to buy it.

Societies

The Royal Horticultural Society, Lindley Library, 80 Vincent Square, London, SW1P 2PE. Tel: 020 7821 3000.
Publishes monthly magazine for members and organizes shows for all levels of gardeners.

Henry Doubleday Research Association (HDRA). Ryton Gardens, Coventry, CV8 3LG. Tel: 02476 303517.
Of interest to all gardeners, but particularly those who wish to learn about organic gardening and composting.

Websites

Most horticultural companies have their own websites now, put www.[name].co.uk and you'll probably get them.
www.rhs.org.uk
The Royal Horticultural Society website
www.hdra.org.uk
See Ryton Gardens above
www.igarden.co.uk/
Internet Gardening Magazine
www.prairienet.org/garden-gate
USA Gardening
www.gardenweb.com/
USA Gardening
www.oldgrowth.org/compost/
All you want to know about composting
www.rbgkew.org.uk/
Kew Royal Botannic Gardens. A good site
www.geocities.com/Avenues/Home-and-Living/Gardening/
USA Forum
www.garden.com
www.gardening.com

About the Author

Roger Wilson has been interested in gardening from an early age. He gained his Higher National Diploma in Landscape and Horticultural Technology in 1985. Roger has worked for a local authority in London, landscape contractors and plant nurseries in the UK and USA. Since 1995 he has been the manager of a garden centre in the Midlands. Roger is a keen member of the National Trust and visits many properties each year with his wife. He also supports English Heritage and visits locally owned private parks and gardens.

INDEX

Note: Page references given in **bold** type indicate the presence of a photograph.

INDEX OF CULTIVAR NAMES

OTHER TITLES AVAILABLE FROM

GMC PUBLICATIONS

BOOKS

GARDENING

Auriculas for Everyone — *Mary Robinson*
Bird Boxes and Feeders for the Garden — Dave Mackenzie
Creating Contrast with Dark Plants — *Freya Martin*
Gardening with Wild Plants — *Julian Slatcher*
Hardy Perennials: A Beginner's Guide — *Eric Sawford*
Orchids are Easy: A Beginner's Guide to their Care and Cultivation — *Tom Gilland*
The Birdwatcher's Garden — Hazel & Pamela Johnson
The Living Tropical Greenhouse: Creating a Haven for Butterflies — John & Maureen Tampion

CRAFTS

American Patchwork Designs in Needlepoint — *Melanie Tacon*
A Beginners' Guide to Rubber Stamping — *Brenda Hunt*
Blackwork: A New Approach — *Brenda Day*
Celtic Cross Stitch Designs — *Carol Phillipson*
Celtic Knotwork Designs — *Sheila Sturrock*
Celtic Knotwork Handbook — *Sheila Sturrock*
Collage from Seeds, Leaves and Flowers — *Joan Carver*
Complete Pyrography — *Stephen Poole*
Contemporary Smocking — *Dorothea Hall*
Creating Colour with Dylon — *Dylon International*
Creating Knitwear Designs — *Pat Ashforth & Steve Plummer*
Creative Doughcraft — *Patricia Hughes*
Creative Embroidery Techniques Using Colour Through Gold — *Daphne J. Ashby & Jackie Woolsey*
The Creative Quilter: Techniques and Projects — *Pauline Brown*
Cross Stitch Kitchen Projects — *Janet Granger*
Cross Stitch on Colour — *Sheena Rogers*
Decorative Beaded Purses — *Enid Taylor*
Designing and Making Cards — *Glennis Gilruth*
Embroidery Tips & Hints — *Harold Hayes*
Glass Painting — *Emma Sedman*
How to Arrange Flowers: A Japanese Approach to English Design — *Taeko Marvelly*
An Introduction to Crewel Embroidery — *Mave Glenny*
Making and Using Working Drawings for Realistic Model Animals — *Basil F. Fordham*
Making Character Bears — *Valerie Tyler*
Making Decorative Screens — *Amanda Howes*
Making Greetings Cards for Beginners — *Pat Sutherland*
Making Hand-Sewn Boxes: Techniques and Projects — *Jackie Woolsey*
Making Knitwear Fit — *Pat Ashforth & Steve Plummer*
Natural Ideas for Christmas: Fantastic Decorations to Make — *Josie Cameron-Ashcroft & Carol Cox*
Needlepoint: A Foundation Course — *Sandra Hardy*
Pyrography Designs — *Norma Gregory*
Pyrography Handbook — *Stephen Poole*
Ribbons and Roses — *Lee Lockheed*
Rubber Stamping with Other Crafts — *Lynne Garner*
Sponge Painting — *Ann Rooney*
Tassel Making for Beginners — *Enid Taylor*
Tatting Collage — *Lindsay Rogers*
Temari: A Traditional Japanese Embroidery Technique — *Margaret Ludlow*
Theatre Models in Paper and Card — *Robert Burgess*
Wool Embroidery and Design — *Lee Lockheed*
Designing and Making Wooden Toys — *Terry Kelly*
Wooden Toy Projects — *GMC Publications*

MAGAZINES

EXOTIC GARDENING · WATER GARDENING · GARDEN CALENDAR · OUTDOOR PHOTOGRAPHY
WOODTURNING · WOODCARVING · FURNITURE & CABINETMAKING
THE ROUTER · BUSINESSMATTERS · THE DOLL'S HOUSE MAGAZINE

The above represents a selection of titles available direct from the Publishers or through bookshops, newsagents and specialist retailers. To place an order, or to obtain a complete catalogue, contact:

GMC Publications,
Castle Place, 166 High Street, Lewes, East Sussex BN7 1XU, United Kingdom
Tel: 01273 488005 Fax: 01273 478606 Email: pubs@thegmcgroup.com
Orders by credit card are accepted